Unbelievable Crimes Volume Nine

Unbelievable Crimes, Volume 9

Daniela Airlie

Published by Daniela Airlie, 2024.

While every precaution has been taken in the preparation of this book, the publisher assumes no responsibility for errors or omissions, or for damages resulting from the use of the information contained herein.

UNBELIEVABLE CRIMES VOLUME NINE

First edition. February 2, 2024.

Table of Contents

Prologue

Welcome to Volume Nine of *Unbelievable Crimes*. In this volume, I'll cover 11 more twisted, macabre tales you've perhaps not heard of.

This book is filled with tales of people who commit (and try to get away with) truly heinous acts, stories so unthinkable you find yourself wondering how on earth they can be true. More than that, this book details the victims and their story, their senseless end, and highlights how, the majority of the time, these people were victims of individuals they already knew.

People they thought they were safe with, people who they ought to have been safe with.

This is a terrifying true crime statistic: over 50% of killings are carried out by someone the victim knows. Some victims perhaps know they are in danger. Abusive relationships, for example, can often foreshadow the victims' fate. But for other cases, such as when someone is murdered by a friend or close family member, they don't see it coming. *Why would they?*

This is such a terrifying thought to me. In their final moments, the victims are all too aware that the person they trusted and cared about is the one ending their life, often in a horrifically brutal way. It reminds me of a saying that goes along the lines of, "The saddest thing about betrayal is that it never comes from your enemies - it comes from those you trust."

In this installment of *Unbelievable Crimes*, I'll cover the case of a con man who duped his girlfriend into not only thinking he had the cure for cancer but also that he was immortal. As well as a fantasist, this man was an emotional manipulator who instigated the death of an innocent woman whose only "wrongdoing" was to reject him.

I also detail the shocking murder of a teenage girl who died at the hands of three teenage boys. The reason for her untimely - and horrific - death makes the case all the more despicable.

Then, I cover the lesser-known case of a spurned lover who took out terrifying revenge on his ex. Her transgression? Another man had taken a picture of her and posted it on social media.

As always, before we begin, I'd like to offer a word of caution about the cases in this book. Some of these chapters include details involving sexual assault, torture, or crimes involving children. Please bear this in mind before reading.

If you're ready, let's delve into Volume Nine.

Murder on the Water

While this case takes place in Florida, it begins in Cincinnati, Ohio, in 1946. Oba Chandler Junior was born to mother Margaret and father Oba Senior. To differentiate between father and son, the younger Oba went by "Obie," a cutesy name that didn't reflect the child's destructive and difficult nature. Even from a very young age, the boy was chaotic, even failing fourth grade for refusing to attend school.

Obie's mother simply had no control over her son, who was showing signs of aggression and a complete disregard for other human beings, much less for authority.

In 1957, just before Obie turned 11, Oba Senior was found hanging in the family home. Helen Chandler, Obie's older sister, had made her way to the basement to collect something when she was met with a sight she'd never be able to erase from her mind: her father hung from the beam.

However, relatives on Oba Senior's side were suspicious at best. They didn't believe their beloved family member would end his own life. They blamed his wife, Margaret, accusing her of killing him. The backlash from Oba's family meant that Margaret would have to step back from attending her late husband's funeral.

Had Margaret attended the funeral, she would have witnessed her son, Obie, jumping on his father's coffin. As the family members scattered dirt on the grave, young Oba Junior jumped onto the coffin as the soil was thrown in. It was a startling sight that would set the foundations for Oba's life of degeneracy and wickedness.

While Oba Senior's family continued to blame Margaret for this death, Margaret pointed her finger at young Oba. She didn't think her son directly killed her husband but rather pushed him toward ending his life with his behavioral issues and aggressive reactions to discipline. Perhaps it was grief talking, or maybe Margaret really did think her son had driven his father to end his life. Either way, there was one thing Margaret knew for a fact: Oba's behavior would only get worse.

Before the youngster turned 18, he racked up 20 arrests for crimes like theft and dealing with counterfeit money. Oba didn't leave his bad behavior behind when he left his teens. It only worsened. The crimes went from what some may call petty and escalated to truly troubling acts of perversion.

In one instance, he was caught touching himself inappropriately while looking into a woman's window, a crime he was arrested for. However, this didn't deter the young man from continuing down a wayward, depraved path, and he would resume his life of crime as soon as he was released from police custody.

From armed robbery to kidnapping, Oba Chandler's spate of criminal activity was getting more and more severe.

Oba's succession of crimes would lead him to Florida, where he would meet like-minded people, individuals like himself who wouldn't think twice about stealing and cheating to get by. In one incident, Oba and a friend carried out a home robbery together, holding a couple at gunpoint while they ransacked their home.

The criminals tied the man up, but Oba had other ideas for the woman. He dragged her into the bedroom and demanded she strip. The terrified woman obliged, fearing for her life if she dared refuse. After all, her attacker was waving a gun toward her as he forced her to remove her clothing. Once she was down to just her underwear, her attacker pushed the barrel of his gun onto her bare skin, moving it back and forth as she cried. It was clear that terrifying this woman brought Oba great pleasure.

While he acted in monstrous ways, Oba was able to mask his true depravity enough to attract a number of women, often seeing multiple women at the same time. He was seen as charming by certain members of the opposite sex, something he used to his advantage over the years. While he never gave his love interests much in the way of stability or loyalty, he was rarely in a situation where he didn't have a girlfriend. More often than not, he had multiple, and he fathered at least eight children by just about as many women.

Oba's innate ability to woo the opposite sex began with his first girlfriend in his teens. She had two children with him, though young Oba joined the Marines shortly after their birth. Upon his return, his philandering ramped up, and these secret relationships would produce even more children.

When Oba eventually left his girlfriend, he was dating a woman from Tampa, Florida, named Barbara. Naturally, he wouldn't remain faithful to her despite asking the woman to marry him. Before the pair could walk down the aisle, Oba had left her for a younger woman named Debra.

Debra wasn't like Barbara - she didn't nag, ask questions, or demand accountability from Oba. This suited him perfectly. By this point, it was the late 80s, and Oba was in his early 40s. Settling down was on the cards - almost.

Oba and Debra married and started a life together as a family. They welcomed a daughter, and Oba had set up his own company called Custom Screens, which helped them pay for a home in Dalton Avenue, Tampa. His successful business also enabled Oba to buy himself an extravagant gift: a sports boat.

The boat served as an escape from family life. Oba would take himself out and cruise the water alone, making as much distance between himself and normality as he could. Having the boat not only gave Oba freedom but also helped him indulge in his persistent need to have extramarital affairs. A "single man" with his own boat was attractive to the young, single women he'd meet at the harbor. Often, they'd agree to head out and watch the sunset with him, which is perhaps a testament to just how harmless and genuine he came across.

If only these women - the ones who got away - knew just how close to danger they were.

Fortunately, many of the women who took Oba up on his offer of a sunset drive in his boat were in groups.

In May 1989, Oba met Canadian tourists Judy Blair and Barbara Mottram. The pair were in a convenience store at Madeira Beach, picking up some groceries, when an older man introduced himself. His name was Dave Posner - or Posno, they weren't sure. The fact that Oba changed his name when talking to two young females shows that his intentions were depraved from the start.

He spun them lines and bragged about himself, but one aspect of his spiel was true: he told them about his business. The two young women were offered a trip on "Dave's" boat the next day, an offer Judy accepted.

The next morning, the pair headed out and zoomed across the water on the boat, which was a fun experience for Judy. Oba - or Dave as he was known to the young woman - then asked if Judy would come back that evening for a sunset jaunt on the boat. He pressured her to bring Barbara along with her, a request Judy agreed to.

However, as night arrived, and Judy met back up with Dave as agreed, he was angry to discover she had turned up alone. Barbra had taken another raincheck on the boat trip - perhaps she had a gut instinct that something wasn't right about the man twice their age wanting to take them both out to the middle of nowhere. Judy didn't get the same vibes, but that was soon to change. His mask didn't just slip - he took it off entirely, revealing the monster that had been lurking beneath all along.

Once Oba had got his victim stranded in the middle of nowhere, with no way to escape, he began forcing himself on her. The young woman was shocked by the aggressive advances the man was making and immediately told him no. "Is sex worth losing your life over?" Oba spat at the terrified woman.

No amount of pleas, crying, or telling him no mattered: Oba was going to carry out his sick attack on Judy. The young woman heartbreakingly tried to appeal to Oba's human side, admitting to him that she was a virgin. She wasn't to know that this would just excite her perverse attacker even more. The sick man forced Judy to the floor of the boat and violated her.

Afterward, Oba returned to the steering wheel. He wasn't the calm, charming man he'd been up until just moments before. He was erratic, manic, and acting like a different person. This scared Judy even more. All she wanted to do was get back on land and flee her abuser as fast as she could. Her friend was waiting for her in the hotel room, and that's what Judy focused her mind on.

Still, her rapist sat beside her, trying to make small talk. Judy pulled her legs to her chest and tried to shield herself from any further attacks. Then, Oba did something peculiar; he raced to the side of the boat and vomited. He didn't just do this once; he threw up multiple times. You may say it was seasickness, though this hadn't plagued Oba before. Perhaps it was guilt at the irreparable damage he'd just done to this young woman, though the more you learn about Oba, the less you may be inclined to believe this theory.

Perhaps it was because he'd just done something seriously reprehensible and illegal and was unable to kill his victim. Oba was forced to let his victim go since she had a friend waiting for her who was able to identify "Dave" as the last person Judy was with. If the two young women had met the man together as he'd requested, he may have killed them both, thus leaving no witnesses.

Once they got back on land, Judy fled back to the safety of her hotel room. Barbara was waiting for her, and she immediately knew something awful had happened. Barbara consoled her friend as best she could, and the next day, they went to the police. Sadly, there wasn't any forensic evidence to be taken. All that Judy could give the police was a detailed and accurate description of her ordeal, plus a comprehensive illustration of what her attacker looked like.

This facial composite was made public by the police, who appealed for witnesses. However, nobody came forward. Oba was free to remain on the streets, though it wouldn't take him long to strike again.

It was June 1, 1989, a mere fortnight since he'd brutally attacked Judy.

Joan Rogers and her teenage daughters, Michelle and Christe, had been vacationing in Tampa. Husband Hal was back in Ohio taking care of the farm while his girls took their first-ever trip out of state.

After a fun-filled vacation, they got lost on their way back home and booked a motel to stay an extra night. The trio bumped into a man who offered them the directions they desperately needed, and he wrote them down on a brochure. "Would you like to take a trip on my boat later this evening?" the seemingly helpful man offered. Joan looked at her girls, who were excited at the prospect of zooming around on a sports boat in Florida. The mother agreed.

Joan, Michelle, and Christe met up with Oba at the dock as planned that evening. Nobody knows how the trip began, if Oba took off his mask immediately, or if he waited until he was far out into the water. What we do know, however, is the tragic outcome.

Oba tied all three victims' hands behind their backs with rope and taped their mouths closed. Their eyes remained uncovered, which provokes a sickening thought: that each victim was able to see the abuse and horrors inflicted upon the others. Oba raped his captives before tying a rope around each of their necks which was attached to a heavy block of concrete. Then, he callously threw them overboard. They were still alive.

It only took a couple of days for the bodies to be found. While Oba had done his best to ensure the victims were dragged to the bottom of the water, nature ensured they didn't stay there. Gasses are released as part of the decomposition process, which caused the bodies to rise to the surface of the water. The heavy blocks were still attached to the victims.

Once the bodies were removed from what Oba hoped was their grave, it became paramount for authorities to identify the victims. It was clear as day that this was a brutal homicide, and the hunt for a triple killer was on. Dental records were able to confirm the identities of the mother and her girls. Husband and father, Hal Rogers, was notified. His whole world - his wife, their daughters, and the life he adored so much - collapsed.

Madeira Beach police appealed for witnesses, and they were inundated with tips. You'd think that this made tracking the killer down easier, but the slough of information the police had to wade through only slowed down the investigation. Still, the lead detective was proactive in his thinking and quickly matched up the rapist from a few weeks prior as likely being the same man who killed the Rogers family.

A deeper look into Judy Blair's horrifying story revealed that there was no "Dave Posner" (or "Posno," as he might have pronounced it) who resided in Tampa Bay. The composite sketch that had been created from Judy's description was redistributed, this time cropping up just about everywhere in the area. Oba Chandler happened upon this sketch, realizing his face was plastered outside convenience stores, on fences, and tacked to the side of buildings. He began panicking.

While Oba certainly wasn't a good husband in the first place, his treatment of Debra only worsened during this time. Perhaps, then, she found a little relief when he fled the family home without so much as a goodbye. Oba returned to his home city of Cincinnati, checking into a motel to plan his next move. The consequences of his depravity were slowly creeping behind him to collect justice, but Oba was going to do whatever it took to evade it.

He made a stressed-out call to one of his now-adult daughters from a previous relationship. Surprisingly, he confessed all. This perhaps wasn't Oba cleansing his soul of the wicked deeds he'd carried out, but more a cry for help out of the situation. His daughter called Debra and told her of her husband's confession.

Sure, Debra had seen the composite sketch - who hadn't? She'd also noticed the uncanny resemblance it had to her husband. Still, when Oba returned home just weeks after fleeing, he denied any knowledge of the attacks, let alone the sketch doing the rounds that just so happened to be his doppelganger.

Life resumed as usual. Debra took Oba at his word and never asked him about his involvement in the rape or murders again. As such, years passed by, and Oba remained a free man.

Still, Oba was acting erratically and was clearly panicked. He told his wife he ought to leave the state, and this didn't prompt Debra to ask questions. Rather, she insisted she go with him. A futile attempt to set up a home in California was made before the couple returned to Tampa Bay.

By this point, Oba's business was no longer the fruitful endeavor it once was. He needed to make money quickly, so he took on a job for the Tampa Police Department, of all places, acting as an informant.

When 1992 rolled around, three years since the murders, the case was about as cold as it could be. Nobody expected it to be solved since there was no solid evidence or leads pointing in a worthwhile direction until the police happened upon a vital clue that had been overlooked. Joan Rogers' car remained parked at the motel they'd booked into, and a more thorough search of it found a brochure with handwriting on it. The style of the writing wasn't Joan's, nor had her daughters penned the directions.

It was a long shot, but the police decided to make the handwriting public to see if anyone recognized it. Nobody truly expected someone to come forward, but they did. A woman who'd used Oba Chandler's business services years earlier recognized the unique style of handwriting as his. The police now had a name. She gave the police the receipt he'd signed for comparison.

Sure enough, the writing matched. But they needed more proof. A palm print from the brochure found in Joan's car was analyzed; it belonged to Oba Chandler. The puzzle pieces were beginning to find themselves being pulled together. The police wanted to gather as much evidence as they could on their suspect before making an arrest. They wanted their case to be airtight. So, they sought to collect any remaining evidence from Oba's boat, but when they traced it, they found he'd sold it right after the murders occurred.

So, law enforcement made the decision to arrest Oba with the small handful of evidence they had. But, they had one last hope - Judy Blair. They reasoned she would be able to recognize her rapist in a lineup, and that's just what she did in the summer of 1992.

His trial for three counts of first-degree murder began in September 1994.

Since Oba confessed all to his daughter, you may expect a similar confession when faced with the evidence against him. Oba didn't confess but instead protested his innocence throughout. Still, he was caught telling lies when he took the stand. For example, to explain why he was out so late the night he killed the mother and daughters, he said his boat had broken down, and he'd made distress calls to the Coast Guard. Calls to the Coast Guard are monitored and recorded - there's no record of Oba calling for help.

Still, Oba would sit and stare at jurors throughout the trial. It seems he was playing mind games - glaring at them while smirking.

Judy Blair was called as a witness and gave a damning testimony against Oba. As did his daughter, who told the jury how her dad confessed to her that he'd killed three women in 1989. Then there was one of Oba's former employees, who testified that Oba came into work on June 1, 1989, tired and groggy. When asked about this, Oba bragged about sleeping with three women mere hours before. These women were, in fact, his three victims.

Oba Chandler was sentenced to death in November 1994. Still, he maintained his innocence, making several appeals against his sentence. Eventually, he said he did have an altercation with Judy on the boat but insisted that the encounter was consensual.

Timescales for being on death row differ, but it's rare for an inmate to be on death row for less than a decade. Oba Chandler's time came in November 2015 while awaiting execution at Florida State Prison. He left a note behind that simply said, "You are killing an innocent man today."

If by now you've thought to yourself, surely there are more victims of Oba Chandler, you'd be right. While he only got sentenced for the Rogers family (he wasn't charged with raping Judy since he'd already received a death sentence), it transpired there's at least one more victim of his depravity.

In 1990, a young woman named Ivelisse Berrios-Beguerisse left her job at the mall one night to discover her car tires had been slashed. The police surmise that the 20-year-old was approached by a "helpful" stranger who they now know to be Oba.

He tied up her hands and feet and taped her mouth, just like the Rogers murders. Again, the eyes remain uncovered.

Just a few hours later, her lifeless body was found by fishermen.

DNA was certainly utilized in 1990, but not to the scale and accuracy it is today. While samples were collected from Ivelisse's body, the technology was unable to find a match at the time. It was only in 2014 that the match to Oba was made. It took almost 24 years for Ivelisse's family to be given some form of closure. They were advised the killer had already been caught and was facing death for his abhorrent crimes.

It's not unreasonable to wonder if - or how many - unsolved murders that took place in Florida in the 80s and 90s could be traced back to Oba Chandler.

The Con Man

This case involves a con man, conspiracy theories, and a successful fashion designer, three things you've probably never seen put together in a sentence before. It culminates in the horrific murder of an innocent woman.

What sounds like a direct-to-video movie plot is, in fact, the true life story of Girly Chew Hossencofft, a woman who found herself entangled with the wrong man. Her choice of love interest unwittingly led her to a world of lies and abuse, ending in her senseless murder.

The story begins in October 1953 in Hollywood, California, when Linda Henning was born. Her mother and father had a tumultuous relationship, which ended when her father left the family home in 1964. By this point, Linda was 11 years old and would be privy to her mother's succession of boyfriends that came in and out of her life.

Linda was a good student, although perhaps more creative than academic. She graduated high school and quickly realized she needed money to get by, so she applied for some modeling jobs for quick cash. She eventually found herself walking the runaways as a sought-after fashion model. This gig brought in enough money for Linda to try to make her hobby and true passion her livelihood - she loved designing clothes. It turns out other women also loved her designs, and she launched her own successful clothing line.

In the 80s, in the midst of her success as a designer, Linda moved to Albuquerque, New Mexico. Here, life would blossom into something Linda could only have imagined growing up; she owned a thriving business, was able to buy a home, and met a man she would eventually become engaged to. Things, for a while, were perfect.

When she wasn't working on her clothing line, Linda had a few hobbies she would indulge in. One of these hobbies was learning about UFOs and aliens. The idea of the unknown and the fact that we may have encountered other life forms intrigued Linda. The Roswell incident was a three-hour drive from Linda's home, where aliens were alleged to have crashed in 1947. She was fascinated by the notion she was so close to the alien encounter.

As well as alternate life forms, Linda was interested in conspiracies. So much so, in the summer of 1999, she booked tickets for a seminar by a conspiracy theorist who believed reptilians rule the world and that shapeshifters with ill intentions walk among us. It was here she'd meet a man she'd fall head over heels for, Diazien Hossencofft.

They bonded over their mutual interest in various conspiracies. Linda was impressed by Diazien, particularly when he told her he was a former CIA agent. He was well-off financially, he told her, since his job entailed curing rich women of cancer. He'd created a vitamin cocktail that he would inject into older women, helping them retain their youth and prevent fatal diseases. Diazien didn't use these miracle injections on himself, though; he didn't need to. He was immortal. Linda was amazed by the man she'd just met and believed every word he told her.

While Linda was intelligent and certainly clever enough to create and sustain a successful business, those who knew her have described her as gullible. Linda's own mother said she would believe the moon was made out of cheese if a boy had told her so.

Diazien Hossencofft, you may not be surprised to hear, wasn't immortal. Nor was he a former CIA operative, nor did he cure cancer. His real name was Armand, and he was a regular - albeit untruthful - man from Texas. However, Linda fell for his lies entirely.

The pair began dating, and Linda broke it off with her fiancé. Diazien promised Linda marriage and a life together. The fact that he was already married to Girly Chew Hossencofft didn't faze the adulterer. In fact, Linda was one of three women Diazien had promised to marry despite the fact he was already married.

Girly, 36, was born in Malaysia in 1963. On a trip to America, she met her husband-to-be, and the pair set up a home in Albuquerque. However, Girly's new life in the USA didn't quite end up being the dreamy existence Diazien promised her it would be. He began abusing her, both physically and emotionally, and Albuquerque Police had responded to at least two calls to the Hossencofft residence to deal with Diazien's violent outbursts toward his wife.

Girly worked as a bank teller, and her colleagues were all too aware of her abusive home life. They felt powerless to help her flee her abuser but would listen to Girly as she confided in them about the horrors she experienced at home. Eventually, after one especially brutal episode, Girly left her husband and filed for divorce in early 1999.

As you can imagine, Diazien didn't take this well. In fact, he threatened to kill Girly if she proceeded with the divorce. It was around this time that all of Diazien's lies began to unravel; his estranged wife discovered he wasn't a doctor as he'd claimed, and she also discovered his birth name wasn't Diazien at all. He'd been a fraud, and Girly simply wanted to get as far away as possible from this dangerous man.

However, her abusive ex was persistent. He showed no signs of letting Girly live her life in peace, so the woman had no choice but to contact the authorities. She told them, chillingly, that if anything ever happened to her, they needed to investigate her husband.

While Diazien was making Girly's life hell, he was simultaneously sweeping Linda Henning off her feet. Linda was so besotted by her new partner that she agreed to take some of Diazien's miracle drugs to enable her to summon huge powers. Linda, at her lover's insistence, also stopped bathing or washing her clothes. This was because she was led to believe she had a chemical imbalance. When the reptiles came to earth, they wanted to attach themselves to the best human candidate possible, Diazien told his lover, and Linda was to become the reptilian queen.

After months of harassment, on September 9, 1999, Girly left her job at the bank and would never be seen alive again.

Her boss, aware of the dangerous predicament she was in with her violent ex, called the police the very next day. It was unlike Girly not to show up for work, even when she was going through a rough time at home. For her to not even call in sick was unfathomable; the bank manager knew something untoward had happened.

Authorities dispatched officers to her home for a welfare check. There was no answer, so they forced their way into her apartment, where they found strange spots of bleach on the carpet. Clearly, someone had wanted to thoroughly clean something up. *Surely, Girly hadn't bleached her own carpets.* The police were immediately suspicious. A further look at the numerous bleached spots found the cleaner or cleaners hadn't been so thorough - they'd left specks of blood behind.

As the investigation into Girly's disappearance began, a workman just outside of Albuquerque made a shocking discovery beside the highway. He found bloodied women's clothing, such as underwear and a blouse. Among the garments was duct tape with strands of hair stuck to it. The police were called, and it seemed like their worst fears had transpired - that Girly had been killed.

Earlier in the year, Girly had notified police to seek out Diazien Hossencofft should anything ever happen to her. On September 12, that's just what they did.

However, by the time they'd got to his house, it was deserted. He'd emptied all his belongings, and he was nowhere to be seen. It seems he'd fled the area as soon as he could. So, the investigation led officers to Linda Henning, Diazien's new girlfriend. When the police spoke to her, Linda insisted she had no idea where Diazien was. In fact, she suggested that she'd likely never see him again. It was a strange interaction and one that wasn't wholly truthful; officers asked if she'd ever met Girly. Linda said they'd never met.

However, as police would later discover, Linda had been to Girly's place of work many times to withdraw money. In fact, Girly had been the teller to hand Linda her money on more than one occasion.

The hunt was on for Diazien Hossencofft.

It didn't take long for investigators to track him down in South Carolina, where, to the surprise of nobody, he was shacked up with another of his girlfriends.

Just like Girly and Linda and the plethora of other women he'd fooled over the years, his latest girlfriend thought she and Diazien were soulmates who were going to get married.

Diazien was arrested and brought back to New Mexico. When interviewed, he denied any knowledge of where his ex was and vehemently rebuked the idea that he'd done anything to her.

Still, there were the garments to be tested for DNA to see if they belonged to Girly. If they did, the police were expecting to find Diazien's DNA on there, too. They were sure of it; after all, if he'd been the one to clean her bloodied carpets, he would surely have done a similarly useless job cleaning the clothing of DNA.

Sure enough, the items of clothing were Girly's, and there was another person's DNA on them. But it didn't belong to Diazien. It was Linda Henning's DNA. Not only that, Linda's long hair was entangled in the evidence. Then, there was the blood at Girly's apartment. Of course, the majority was Girly's spilled blood, but some of it belonged to Linda, too.

Linda's home was swarmed by law enforcement, and she was arrested. A search of her home uncovered some gruesome finds: two guns and a Japanese sword hidden in her garage. The sword was of particular interest, and the police were able to trace it back to the buyer, Diazien Hossencofft. The fantasist had bought it the same day Girly vanished.

Weeks later, Diazien was captured again by authorities and arrested on suspicion of first-degree murder. The investigation between Linda and Girly also uncovered that Girly had been her bank teller at least once, thus demolishing her lie about never meeting her.

You'd expect Diazien to deny all culpability or knowledge. To everybody's surprise, he admitted to planning his wife's murder but denied murdering her. Bizarrely, Diazien claimed that he'd planted Linda's blood in Girly's apartment to scupper the investigation, not to incriminate her. He kept on with his insistence he had no idea where the body was. However, to avoid the death penalty, he pleaded guilty to the murder of his wife in exchange for a 60-year sentence to be served in Wyoming.

Linda's trial took place in October 2002, and due to the vast amount of evidence against her, she was looking at the death penalty. Despite there being no body, there was enough forensic evidence to agree that, beyond a reasonable doubt, Linda had murdered Girly. She was found guilty of first-degree murder, kidnapping, and tampering with evidence. She narrowly avoided a death sentence but was handed the closest thing: over 70 years in jail.

With it being over 20 years since Girly was killed, you may wonder why a body still hasn't been recovered. The answer to that may lie in some rumors that plagued Linda throughout the trial: that she'd eaten Girly.

The police investigating the case spoke to a number of people as possible witnesses, some of whom admitted that Linda had confessed to consuming the victim. If this is the case, Girly and her family will never get the burial she deserves.

However, there are people who believe that Linda is innocent. The theory is that Diazien is the true killer and did his best to implicate Linda after slaying his wife. The fact that Linda was offered some very attractive plea bargains before her trial, all of which she rejected, may suggest that she wanted to be found guilty. That way, Diazien could be off the hook. She was, after all, well and truly under his spell.

A Curious Abduction

In early November 2016, Sherri Papini suddenly vanished near her home in California.

Immediately, the race was on to find her alive. As the days passed, statistics weren't on Sherri's side: most missing adults are found within 24 hours of vanishing. Around 90% are found within two days. If the person is missing for longer than a week, that percentage plummets to less than 5%.

Born Sherri Louise Graeff on June 11, 1982, Sherri had a tumultuous few years as an adolescent. When she was 18, she reportedly burglarized her father's home. Her mother also alleged that Sherri was prone to self-harm but was doing so, intending to blame her mother for the injuries.

Though these are truly troubling accusations, Sherri's behavior seemed to stabilize as she got older. She met her husband, Keith, while in middle school, and they were one another's first kiss. However, the pair would grow apart and lose touch for a number of years, reuniting when they were in their 20s.

They began dating once again and soon found themselves in love. Sherri would call Keith her "best friend" and boast of how they were a "perfect couple." Keith felt the same way, and the loved-up pair got married in 2009 and had two children together. They settled in Redding, California, and their life was as picture-perfect as you can imagine for a young family.

Sherri's true crime tale began while she was out on a jog in November 2016. This wasn't unusual for Sherri, but when she'd been gone several hours and hadn't been replying to Keith's messages, he knew something was wrong. He waited a while before using a location tracker on his phone to find Sherri's phone. The location verified his initial thoughts that something was wrong: her phone was on the side of the road less than a mile away from the family home.

Keith called the police, and Sherri's phone was recovered. But that was all they had - there were no leads or evidence. The trail ended there. The hours passed, and Keith was hopeful his wife would turn up and walk through the door. Surely, there was an innocent explanation to all this, he thought. Some misunderstanding or strange turn of events would explain his wife losing her phone and taking off.

However, hours turned into days. The case made the news, with appeals for any information proving to be unfruitful. It was excruciating for Keith, who, although he didn't say it out loud, knew that the more time passed, the less likely it would be they'd find Sherri. He had to maintain a level of composure for their children, though this was no easy task. He was a bundle of anxiety.

Then, three weeks after the woman had vanished, there was an unexpected break in the case. Nobody expected Sherri to simply turn up, but that's just what happened. She was found on a highway 140 miles away from her family home. She was in a terrible state; there was no denying it. Her wrists still had binding around them. She clearly hadn't been fed; she was close to emaciated. Her hair was unkempt; what hair she had left. Whoever had taken her chopped her once-blonde locks off.

Sherri had seemingly endured violence at the hands of her captor or captors, too. She was covered in bruises and had sustained several injuries, including a broken nose. She'd also been "branded" on her shoulder. When she was finally reunited with Keith, he was shocked at how "intense" her injuries were. Not to mention, Sherri didn't look like her usual self. She was beyond thin, her long hair had been hacked off, and she was acting strangely.

You can forgive the woman for her strange behavior after such a traumatizing ordeal, but the police were suspicious of Sherri almost as soon as she turned back up. She was clearly not keen on speaking with the police, preferring to heal from her emotional and physical turmoil in the confines of her family home. She didn't want to court attention or have her case looked into too thoroughly.

Sherri's inconsistency in the story she gave police also caused law enforcement to raise their eyebrows. Initially, she claimed her captors wanted to traffic her. The more Sherri was questioned, the more bizarre her story became.

According to Sherri, she was bundled into a black SUV by two Hispanic women. Her captors had thrown her into a closet in an unknown location and chained her up. Her injuries were suffered when the women took turns torturing her, beating and tormenting their captive for their own enjoyment.

The story was frightening, to say the least. It was also not making much sense; why did the women release Sherri when law enforcement wasn't onto them? They seemingly gained nothing from their three-week assault on the woman. It was also noted that when police found Sherri's phone, it wasn't smashed or thrown somewhere hidden. It was neatly laid down with her headphones tidily placed on top.

Still, law enforcement worked to find the two women responsible for Sherri's ordeal. Detectives' investigation took them to other states, including Michigan, and the FBI aided in the case. Still, there was no sign of the two gun-wielding women who'd abducted Sherri.

Years passed, and although the case seemed cold, the police were still working on cracking the case in the background. They tested the clothing Sherri had on the day she was found and were alarmed to discover there was no other female DNA on there - just male. Sherri hadn't mentioned she'd been in contact with any man during her stint in captivity. In September 2019, the DNA was sent for familial testing.

Familial DNA searches are often carried out as a supplemental investigative tool when the evidence has dried up, or all leads have been probed. Familial DNA searches serve to pinpoint potential relatives of a possible suspect. It's likely the police carried this testing out to rule suspects out, not find new ones. It turns out they managed to do the latter. It led them to Sherri's ex-boyfriend.

In August 2020, the ex was brought in for questioning. The story he had for the police was astounding.

He told detectives he'd known Sherri since they were in their teens, having had a relationship with her when they were younger. According to her ex, Sherri contacted him after a lengthy period of not talking. The unexpected contact led to the woman telling her ex that she was in an abusive relationship - an extremely vicious one filled with violence and rape. She told her former lover that she wanted to escape, and after hearing her story, the ex quickly drove to her and picked her up.

On the way back to his home, Sherri lay in the back of her ex's car and slept. Her behavior once she arrived at his apartment was that of a person who was struggling; she ate little. She chopped her hair off.

Then, she made a startling request: she asked her ex to hurt her. The man was clearly shocked by the ask but did as Sherri asked anyway. He'd never done it before, but he cracked her across the nose to injure her, just as she'd asked him to.

The ex's version of events - as crazy as they sounded - was more believable than Sherri's version. She was again questioned, though the police didn't outright tell her that they'd spoken to her ex. They warned her, once again, that lying to a federal agent is a crime. With that in mind, they asked her about the DNA on her clothing. It matched an old boyfriend of hers. Still, Sherri denied meeting any ex and kept up the story involving the two Hispanic women.

Sherri didn't know that her ex had been asked to take a polygraph test regarding his version of events. He passed. Sherri's hoax was all but fully exposed, yet she still insisted it was a legitimate adduction.

The investigator tried to nudge Sherri into telling them the truth, eventually advising her that her ex had told them everything. Not only that, but he provided the police with information nobody else could know.

In March 2022, Sherri was arrested, and the police put it to her that she had such a drastic weight loss because she ate so little while living with her ex. The injury to her nose was from a hockey stick she'd asked her ex to hit her with. Six weeks later, she admitted they were right: it was all a hoax. Days later, her husband Keith filed for divorce and sought full custody of their children.

He called himself "an idiot" for staying with Sherri and believing her abduction lies.

Sherri was sentenced in September 2022 and was handed 18 months behind bars. She was also given a fine of just over $300,000.

Aside from Sherri's family and loved ones, there were also other people who felt let down by her actions. Her local community had spent hours upon hours looking for her in the days after she vanished and felt duped by her and her story after she was "released" by her captors. Then, there were the Hispanic women who were wrongly suspected as part of the police investigation. After all, the description Sherri gave of her abductors allowed police to create a sketch of the criminals' likenesses. This ended up with a number of innocent individuals getting drawn into the investigation needlessly.

Sherri was apologetic for her actions after her guilty verdict. She agreed she was guilty of "lying and dishonor" and said she was accepting all responsibility for her actions. The only thing Sherri didn't offer was a reason why she did what she did; what provoked her to do such a thing? Was the stress of life so bad she wanted an escape but changed her mind after three weeks? Or, as some others suggest, did she want attention?

In this case, sadly, I doubt we'll ever know.

The Confession vs DNA

Teenage murder cases are a tragic yet prevalent category of true crime cases. In these instances, young lives are cruelly snuffed out to fulfill twisted killers' kicks. These young victims had their whole lives ahead of them, decades that were snatched from them senselessly. Nicole van den Hurk's case is one such tragic tale.

Nicole was born on July 4, 1980, in Germany. Her mother, Angelika, separated from Nicole's biological father and entered a relationship with Ad van den Hurk, whom she ended up marrying. The child adopted her stepfather's surname, and the van den Hurks settled in the Netherlands shortly after.

However, the family's once-idyllic life crumbled after just a few years. The van den Hurks, once so in love, ended their relationship acrimoniously in the late 80s. Angelika lost custody of Nicole to Ad, who had already assumed legal guardianship over the child prior to their split.

Tragedy would strike again for Nicole when Angelika killed herself in 1995. By this point, teenage Nicole wasn't living with her stepfather but had moved in with her grandmother, who resided in Eindhoven in the Netherlands.

Reeling from her mother's sudden and tragic death, Nicole was given comfort and support by her immediate family. To keep her mind busy and to ensure the teenager didn't get swamped by the sadness her mother's death brought her, she got a part-time job at the local shopping mall.

On October 6, 1995, Nicole headed out early on her bike to make it to her morning shift on time. This was one of Nicole's first jobs, and she was known to always be on time. Despite her young age, she was punctual and would never show up late, let alone miss a shift. However, Nicole didn't make it to work on that cold October morning.

She didn't make it back home, either.

Worried sick, her grandmother alerted authorities, who set out searching for the girl. It took around 12 hours for the police to make a discovery, and it wasn't promising in the slightest: Nicole's bike had been tossed carelessly in the Dommel River.

Immediately, her family knew someone had taken her; Nicole was always on time and had never run away before. Despite the stresses she'd been through in the previous five years - her parent's divorce, the subsequent custody battle, and the loss of her mother - they knew she'd never simply take off.

However, this was the theory that was being put to the family. It was suggested to the van den Hurks that Nicole had run off back to Germany, where she was born, to reunite with her biological father. Her stepfather, Ad, scoffed at this idea. He knew she had no interest in doing this, and he was the only father she knew. Wherever Nicole was, she didn't go there willingly, the family knew that much.

Then, almost a fortnight later, on October 19, another macabre clue appeared. It was Nicole's backpack. It was found washed up near Eindhoven's canal. This triggered a wider scout of the canal and river, with a search party also trawling the nearby forests to look for any evidence. The search was carried out multiple times over several weeks, but there were simply no clues to be uncovered.

Four weeks with no leads turned into five, which turned into six. The van den Hurk family were beside themselves with anxiety, hoping that Nicole would walk through the front door while slowly accepting that the chances of that happening were getting slimmer and slimmer each day. By week seven, however, there was a big - and heartbreaking - crack in the case.

On November 22, 1995, a body was found by a person taking a stroll in the woods that divided the towns of Mierlo and Lierop. The shocked passerby could clearly see the young female had been beaten and stabbed prior to their untimely end. The police were called, and the brutalized body was identified as Nicole's.

The subsequent autopsy revealed that Nicole had been raped before she'd been killed. Her jaw was fractured, she'd been beaten around the head, and her fingers had defense wounds. Her ribs had been fractured. It was determined that she'd died after bleeding out from the multiple stab wounds she endured.

Nicole's body had been disposed of in an area not far from her grandmother's home. She was heartbreakingly so close to safety when she was killed.

The investigation began, and the hunt was on for the monster who carried out this atrocious act of depravity. The police, shortly after Nicole's disappearance, had received a call from a man confessing he knew who killed the teenager.

Frustratingly, the call was cut off before a name or any other information could be divulged. Still, the police actually had managed to create a shortlist of potential suspects, starting with a tip from an Eindhoven woman named Celine Hartogs.

Celine told law enforcement that she knew then men - there was more than one - who'd killed Nicole. The woman had been arrested for a separate crime to do with drug trafficking and claimed that the men who'd forced her to smuggle heroin were the same men who'd murdered Nicole.

However, after putting the puzzle pieces together, the police found they just didn't fit. They viewed her claims as baseless and decided that they did nothing but skew the investigation. Celine's evidence was dismissed.

By this point, media outlets were offering monetary rewards for any information on Nicole's murderer or murderers. Still, investigators were at a loss.

Almost a year after Nicole had been killed, the police brought in her stepfather, Ad, for questioning. They also brought in her stepbrother, Andy van den Hurk. It was a stretch since there was no real evidence pointing law enforcement to them, but the police had no other avenues to turn. The father and son were interviewed, but the police had no choice but to clear them of any wrongdoing. There wasn't one shred of evidence to suggest they were involved in the killing.

By now, it was summer 1996, and the case was just about ice cold. The police knew this and decided to cut the number of men they had on the investigation team. This was, sadly, the beginning of the authorities acknowledging that it was unlikely the culprit would ever be found, let alone brought to justice. They simply couldn't justify the funding anymore.

Years passed, and with nobody really looking into the case, it was largely forgotten about. Not by the van den Hurks, of course, but law enforcement and the media had moved on.

Then, in 2004, a cold case team sparked a renewed interest in the murder. Sadly, this team was also cut shortly after it was announced. Yet again, Nicole van den Hurk's case was buried.

Seven years later, a breakthrough occurred. Someone had made a full confession to the murder on social media. It was someone the police had already spoken to: Nicole's stepbrother, Andy.

By 2011, he'd moved from the Netherlands to the UK to start a new life. That spring, he posted an alarming status on his social media page, admitting he killed Nicole, which caused him to be arrested by the British police. Andy was detained until March 30, when he was sent back to the Netherlands to face justice for the murder.

Only he wouldn't face justice. He was released five days after returning home.

The police had no evidence to tie Andy to the murder; they had nothing but a flimsy social media post confessing to it. This was nowhere near enough to arrest him.

Once released, Andy would admit he'd lied about killing Nicole. He didn't do it for attention or to fulfill some strange kick; he did it to reignite law enforcement's interest in finding the true killer.

Of course, Andy knew it could have backfired horribly. If the police wanted to simply put someone behind bars for the crime to close the case, they had the opportunity right there. However, Andy's motivation was to prompt the police to exhume Nicole and test her for DNA. Surely, Andy thought, the advances in technology could help snare his sister's killer.

The strange, albeit successful, plan did end up encouraging law enforcement to dig Nicole's body up. The DNA found on her was re-tested, and the results whittled the suspects down to two men: the DNA of her boyfriend at the time and the DNA of an unknown person.

The search was on to find out who the second person's DNA was.

Detectives decided they would look into similar cases that had occurred in the area both before and after Nicole's murder. In doing so, they came across the brutal crimes of a man called Jos de G.

In 2000, near the same area where Nicole was found, a young woman was pulled off her bike and raped at knifepoint. Thankfully, the woman survived and was able to identify her attacker. Jos de G was convicted of the twisted crime and was sent to prison. By the time the police matched the similarities between this case and Nicole's case, Jos de G was again free.

In fact, Jos had been found guilty of three rapes in his lifetime. Each crime carried a paltry sentence, meaning his time behind bars never amounted to much at all. He was ordered to seek compulsory treatment for his sick urges, but it became clear that these sessions didn't help quell the man's desire for violence and degradation toward the opposite sex.

In order to tie Jos to the crime, the police compared a previously submitted sample of his DNA with the evidence found on Nicole's body. It matched. Not only did law enforcement have a positive semen match connecting Jos to the crime, but they also found one of his hairs on the victim.

A deeper investigation into his whereabouts the morning of Nicole's vanishing found he had fled his girlfriend's home after a bitter argument. He was around the area where the teenager had vanished.

You would think all of this would make the case clear cut: Jos de G was guilty. It was harder to prove than you might imagine. The DNA was all the prosecution had to convict the man, but his defense team managed to make it a controversial piece of evidence.

The semen was found in two locations: the genital area and the victim's underwear. At his 2014 trial for Nicole's murder, Jos' defense argued that the body had been exposed to the harsh outdoors and bacteria for seven weeks before being discovered. He argued that this would cause high levels of contamination for the DNA found on Nicole.

Jos' defense lawyer also argued that there was another man's DNA on the victim's body, which was from her boyfriend at the time. They suggested this potential suspect was never looked into adequately.

The defense team put forward that there was every chance Jos had consensual intercourse with Nicole before her murder and even brought up her prior dating history to prove how this was plausible. Due to Jos' transient lifestyle in 1995, it was probable he had sex with Nicole and couldn't remember the interaction, his defense suggested.

In the summer of 2014, murder charges against Jos were dropped. Instead, he was charged with rape and manslaughter.

In 2015, Jos' new trial began. By this point, a witness had come forward to claim that Jos had confessed to them that he'd killed a girl years ago. He'd not named the girl during this confession, and the fact that he was in a mental health facility while he made the admission dampened the strength of it. Jos' defense would state the individual who had come forward with this information did so to claim the monetary reward for helping snare Nicole's killer.

Despite the defense team working overtime to show Nicole as promiscuous and claiming her interaction with Jos was consensual, the court wasn't swayed. In November 2016, he was found guilty of raping Nicole but absolved of the manslaughter charge against him.

This sentence was appealed, and in October 2018, the manslaughter charge was upheld, and he was handed 12 years behind bars for his crimes.

A Pact with the Devil

Elyse Pahler was just 15 years old when her life was torn from her in one of the most barbaric, brutal ways you can imagine. *Why*? Because three teen boys decided they wanted to sacrifice her in order to pacify Satan. If they got in Satan's good books, they assumed that they'd be earning themselves a one-way ticket to hell. Bizarrely, that's exactly what they wanted.

Born in 1980 in Arroyo Grande, California, to mom Lisanne and dad David, Elyse was the eldest of the four Pahler children. The family was close-knit, with any tiffs or arguments forgotten about almost as soon as they erupted. The clan was a big part of their little town's community, especially within the church.

Elyse was known to be a creative soul, enjoying painting in particular. As she entered her teens, her circle of friends grew, and her desire to be sociable swelled, too. However, some of the youngsters' social circle wasn't exactly the crowd her mother and father had hoped their daughter would befriend. Still, Lisanne and David let their eldest have the freedom and space she craved while still doing their best to keep an eye on her. Elyse was your typical freshman, and her parents knew that smothering her could cause her to rebel in dangerous ways.

The teen still spent quality time with her family, enjoying dinners and movie nights together on the sofa. On July 22, 1995, the Pahlers were having a movie marathon, watching films late into the night. Elyse took a phone call from a friend at around ten that evening, and after hanging up, they called back a short while later. From what her parents could tell, it seemed like a normal conversation between Elyse and her friends, but they noticed her mood change after the second call.

"I'm tired; I think I'll head to bed," she said, leaving the family to finish watching the movie without her.

Again, this wasn't out of the ordinary. Teenagers are known to need plenty of sleep, and despite it being Saturday night, Elyse didn't feel like staying up late. At least, that's what her parents presumed. In reality, the teen had formulated a plan to sneak out, something plenty of teens have done (and gotten away with) throughout history. Elyse had snuck out many times before; sometimes, she got away with it, and sometimes she was caught out. Either way, she was always back before the sun came up.

When the Pahlers finished their final film, they, too, decided to call it a night and headed to bed. David quickly checked in on his daughter, expecting to see her sound asleep in bed. Instead, he discovered the wily teen had rumpled her pillows beneath her blanket to make it look like she was bundled underneath. She'd snuck out, causing David and Lisanne to have yet another conversation about what they could do to straighten their daughter out.

They weren't harsh disciplinarians, but they didn't want their child's behavior getting out of control. Deciding to go to sleep and speak with Elyse in the morning when she was home, the couple retreated to their bedroom.

When they awoke the next day, likely full of stern words for their daughter, they were dealt a devastating blow when they opened Elyse's bedroom door. She wasn't there. Pillows were still in the place she ought to be. David raced to the phone and called 911.

The search for Elyse started off intense, but it fizzled out quickly. There was no evidence, no leads, and there were no clues left behind. Much to the Pahlers' dismay and upset, the case was pretty much cold immediately.

Months passed by and there was no fresh evidence and no communication from Elyse. The family had no choice but to face the very real prospect that she was never coming home again. Almost a year passed before there was a crack in the case; it wasn't just a small crack, either. It blew the whole case wide open.

On March 16, 1996, a nervous teenager entered the Arroyo Grande Police Department and wanted to speak to somebody. He had something important he wanted to get off his chest. There was no way the interviewing investigators could prepare themselves for what Royce Casey was about to tell them.

A renewed connection with his faith prompted the teenager to confess that he was one of three boys to end Elyse Pahler's life. He, along with Jacob Delashmutt and Joseph Fiorella, lured Elyse to meet them before raping, torturing, and killing her.

Shockingly, the murder wasn't a spontaneous idea. The three boys had meticulously planned it for weeks leading up to that fateful July evening. Royce told the police that the trio were part of a heavy metal band, and this led them to want to learn more about the occult. In turn, this prompted them to connect with others online who also had an interest in witchcraft and the supernatural. According to the 17-year-old, he and his friends got talking to another occultist who informed them that their band could be one of the most famous bands to exist - all they had to do was please Satan.

When they asked what kind of things they could do to please Satan, their online acquaintance told them to "commit the ultimate sin." The misguided user elaborated, saying killing a young virgin would equate to ultimate sin. The three boys didn't hesitate - they began making plans right away. It was a small price to pay - ending the life of another human - in order to find fame and riches with their band, aptly named *Hatred*.

Joseph Fiorella made no secret of the fact that he had a crush on Elyse. Nothing came of his interest in the teenager; they ran in different circles for the most part. So, he suggested slaying her in order to please Satan. She was perfect for their sacrifice, he reasoned. She was a virgin with blonde hair and blue eyes. For unclear reasons, the boys thought that those physical traits made the girl more "pure" and, therefore, more attractive to Satan.

For weeks, Royce, Jacob, and Joseph perfected their plan. They began stalking their soon-to-be victim, trying to understand her routine and figure out what might stand in the way of them being able to carry out the killing successfully.

When they called Elyse the night they killed her, they promised her some marijuana. Like a lot of teens, Elyse had indulged in the odd smoke of a joint here and there, though this was about the extent of her experimenting. She, by all accounts, didn't seek it out but would smoke it in a social setting. This fact may have found its way back to the three boys, and they decided to dangle the promise of cannabis to lure her to them.

Royce guided the police to Elyse's body in a eucalyptus grove less than half a mile from her family home. By this point, a year after her murder, her body was partially mummified. It was clear to see, despite her decomposed state, that Elyse's death had been violent. She had multiple stab marks and ligature marks around her neck.

The police arrested Royce, as well as 16-year-old Jacob Delashmutt and 15-year-old Joseph Fiorella. The three were all questioned, and it didn't take long for the police to realize that all of them were heavily involved. Royce insisted the plan, for the most part, had been put together by Jacob and Joseph.

After agreeing to join the boys to get high, they took Elyse to the eucalyptus grove in a nearby mesa. The violence didn't begin right away; the teenagers passed around a joint and enjoyed small talk for a while. Tragically, not one of the teenagers decided to back out or call the vile plan off, even after laughing and joking with the intended victim.

Suddenly, Jacob took his belt off and wrapped it around Elyse's neck. He pulled it tight to restrain her as the three boys sexually violated her. After they'd raped her, the victim was begging for help. The callous boys didn't care; they began to torture her. Jacob again began pulling on the belt tight around the teenager's throat while Joseph stabbed her around the neck. Then, Royce and Jacob took turns with the hunting knife to stab the girl repeatedly. They passed the knife to one another, much like they had with the joint earlier, laughing at Elyse's pleas for mercy. When she realized they had none, she started asking for her mom.

After carrying out multiple stabs all over her body, the boys grew tired of the knife and began beating the girl as she lay on the floor. Elyse prayed as her murderers stomped and kicked her as she bled out. In a sick display, purportedly to gain favor with Satan, the trio again raped Elyse.

The three boys were charged with first-degree murder. Joseph Fiorella pled guilty, which saw him receive at least 26 years in jail. Royce Casey pleaded no contest and got a minimum of 21 years. Jacob Delashmutt pleaded no contest and got a minimum of 26 years in jail.

As you can imagine, David and Lisanne were full of rage and upset at the sickening way their daughter's life had ended. They needed more accountability; simply jailing the perpetrators wasn't enough. They wanted to pinpoint and eradicate the very thing that led to their daughter's murder, which they felt was a heavy metal band named Slayer. The boys listened to their music and, according to the Pahler parents, wouldn't have carried out the killing if their music didn't exist.

So, they sued the band: once in 2000, when it was thrown out of court, and again a few years later, which was also dismissed.

Jacob, years after his sentencing, was interviewed in jail. He rebuffed the Pahlers' belief that the band influenced them to murder. He claimed that Joseph's obsession with Elyse was the real driving force behind the killing. No amount of heavy metal music or shocking lyrics can force a person to kill - the seed already has to be there.

Despite being just 15 at the time of the killing, Jacob said Joseph was possessive over Elyse, even though they weren't in a relationship. He wanted her desperately, and when he figured she didn't want him, he didn't want anyone else to have her either. So, she had to die. The idea of "pleasing Satan" was allegedly a ruse Joseph hid behind in order to rally the boys into murdering Elyse with him.

Royce Casey spent 20 years in jail and seemingly made the most of the opportunities handed to him there. He got his GED, keenly participated in various rehab programs, and was aiming for a degree in psychology. His "model prisoner" status led to him being granted parole in 2022, despite Governor Gavin Newson denying Royce parole a year prior.

Joseph and Jacob remain detained.

Royce has since described Elyse as a "wonderful" person. He acknowledges he caused her immense pain and suffering and claims she was a victim of his need to be seen as tough and violent by his peers. He added that he's grown as a person while he served his time and has learned to accept himself.

For a parent to outlive their child is an unimaginable weight to bear. For their child to leave this world in such a brutal, violent, and wicked way would leave a wound that no amount of time would ever come close to healing. Still, the Pahlers didn't object to Royce's release, perhaps a testament to their strength of character.

Prom Night Massacre

Pastor Bob Lee Pelley and his new wife, Dawn, found themselves trying to merge their newly blended family in the smoothest way possible.

Both Bob and Dawn had been through the trauma of losing their spouses but were lucky enough to find love again, with five children between them to consider. They set up a home together in Lakeville, Indiana, in the 80s, integrating their respective clan as one big family.

Bob had a boy and a girl, Jeff and Jacque. Dawn had Jessie, Janel, and Jolene, the three J's that comprised her girls. As you can imagine, the five youngsters didn't make it plain sailing for their parents. Squabbles and arguments sometimes ensued; be it Bob and Dawn disagreeing over parenting style, the children opposing their step-parent's demands, or the youngsters having frustration with one another, the blended family could often butt heads.

However, on the outside, the Pelleys were picture-perfect. The children were kind and polite, and the parents were well-respected within the community. Parishioners were able to meet with Bob and his clan on Sundays, and they'd always remark what a great family he had.

By 1989, Bob's son Jeff was teetering the cusp of adulthood. He was 17, and although he was still a child, he behaved like the typical high school senior he was. Jeff had recently sought out independence, rebelling against the Pelley family's desire for a close-knit team. This isn't abnormal for an adolescent boy, although Jeff did start acting out in other ways, too.

Petty theft was Jeff's rebellion method of choice. He stole money from a home in the neighborhood along with some CDs. It's not like Jeff needed either; if he wanted something, most of the time, all he had to do was ask. That's not to say the teen was just handed any materialistic things he wanted, but Bob and Dawn would have worked with Jeff to see that he could earn the cash to buy the things he wanted.

It was important to Bob, in particular, that the Pelley kids were well-behaved. After all, their actions - good or bad - reflected on pastor Bob. For Jeff to do something as dishonest as stealing from neighbors brought great shame and embarrassment to the father. These weren't the morals he stood for and contradicted what he preached. So, Jeff had to be punished.

The punishment - to anyone who isn't a teen - isn't unfairly harsh: Jeff was forbidden from going to prom night after parties. He was fine attending the prom itself, but he was to come straight home afterward. As you can imagine, this punishment went down like a lead balloon. Jeff was upset. Add to the fact that Jeff also got his car privileges removed, and you have one very frustrated and upset teen.

Jeff protested, screamed, and yelled at his father. The punishment, to Jeff, didn't fit the crime. The crime, however, was technically punishable by law, but to the teenager, his father was being wildly unreasonable. Bob would drive his son to and from prom to avoid any notion of him taking off and partying.

Prom night was held on a warm April evening in 1989. One of Jeff's school friends dropped by before heading to prom to see the Pelleys and noticed there was a tense atmosphere in the usually welcoming household. In particular, Jeff seemed unhappy. He wasn't up for talking much, nor did he appear to be excited about going to prom.

Still, he seemed to fix his demeanor by the time he headed to prom. Jeff called his date to let her know he would be a little late in picking her up. It seems his car was having issues, and the teen had to stop off at a gas station to get under the hood and get the vehicle running again. He eventually managed to pick up Darla, and they drove to dinner before making their way to the big event. However, Bob was nowhere in sight, despite his assertion that Jeff would not have access to his car and that he would be driving him to and from prom.

It seemed Bob had relented in his punishment. You only get one prom, after all.

Jeff and Darla had a fun night at the dance, which was followed by a game of bowling. A bunch of seniors met at the alley, and then a small group headed back to one of the gang's houses to end the night, including Jeff and Darla. The friend's plan was to wake up the next day and head to a theme park in Chicago.

The following morning, they headed out and enjoyed a day riding roller coasters and eating cotton candy. Jeff didn't seem to be acting any different from normal, though Darla did recall he said something strange. "I have a feeling something bad has happened at home," he told his girlfriend.

Jeff was right. Something awful *had* happened at the Pelley household.

If we rewind back to the prom day, around mid-afternoon, Jeff's classmate Crystal was at home waiting for Bob and Dawn to drive over and see her prom dress. The Lakeville community was close like that, with the Pelleys, in particular, finding it easy to make friends since they were a well-known family within the area. The couple wouldn't promise to come over and then just not turn up, but that's just what they'd done to Crystal. Disappointed, she took herself to the Pelley's house before heading to prom, but nobody answered the door.

It was a warm, sunny spring evening, but the home had the blinds closed. This was strange, but Crystal didn't have much time to question it since she had her prom night to attend. The Pelley's neighbor also noticed that the family had closed their blinds unusually early. He mowed his lawn and carried out some outdoor chores, looking over at the Pelley home to see if everything was okay. The basement light of the Pelleys stayed on all night, though, which was another oddity the neighbor picked up on.

They'd have to ask Bob if everything was okay when they saw him at church the next day. However, the pastor never made it to his Sunday service. Families flocked to the church, awaiting Bob, but he didn't turn up. If Bob was sick or something unfortunate had happened, he would make sure the community knew. The parishioners decided to knock on the Pelley's door and make sure everything was okay.

They tried to peek through the blinds, but they were shut tight. One community member had a spare key, which was used to gain entry to the home. What the concerned neighbors would walk in on was beyond their wildest nightmares: Bob, surrounded by his own blood, in the entrance hallway. He had visible gunshot wounds, and it was abundantly clear he'd been laid dead for some time.

A group of the men searched the Pelley home to make sure the killer or killers had gone and to see if there were any survivors. They made their way to the basement, where they'd be met with another sickening sight: Dawn, lying dead between Janel and Jolene. Again, each victim had been shot at close range with a gun.

The police were called, and the hunt for the person responsible began. It was noted that three of the five children weren't home at the time of the murders. It was considered that the culprit had kidnaped Jeff, Jacque, and Jessie, or worse, killed them and concealed their bodies elsewhere.

With all options being weighed up, the police and forensics team got to work searching the Pelley property. What they found would suggest the Pelleys were shot with their own shotgun. It was noticeably missing from where it should have been mounted on the wall, and a shell discovered at the macabre scene would confirm that the family had been slain with Bob's gun.

Later that day, nine-year-old Jessie arrived home from a sleepover. The youngster noticed lots of cars and people at her home, and despite her young age, she knew something terrible had happened. Her young mind couldn't possibly consider just how terrible it was.

There was no way to break it to the young girl easily. She was told the truth about what had happened to her family, and as you can imagine, the child's world was turned upside down. Her mother, her stepfather, and her two sisters had been ripped from her overnight.

Still, despite her state of shock, Jessie was able to tell the police that Jeff was with his friends at the theme park, and Jacque was staying at a friend's house. The police tracked the two missing Pelleys down, and they were also informed of the horrifying news.

By the time Jeff got back to Lakeville, investigators had already had a day to do some digging. They'd spoken to friends and neighbors of the Pelleys, and they were aware that Bob had been doing his best to discipline his wayward son. They discovered he'd forbid his son from using the car and that Jeff was supposed to go to his prom and then go straight home. Bob was the one who was due to drop Jeff off and pick him up. Those who knew Bob suggested that the father wouldn't have dropped the punishment, certainly not after Jeff had been caught stealing.

In fact, one of Bob's friends told the police how the fed-up father amended Jeff's car engine to render it undrivable until his punishment was over. His friends stressed that Bob was doing everything he could to get Jeff back on a good path, and to waive his penalty for thieving would be out of character for Bob.

The police now had a suspect with a motive. Jeff was subsequently interviewed with his grandparents in the room. He insisted his father had dropped his punishment and allowed him to drive to prom and go to the theme park with his friends. When asked about the murder, Jeff insisted he didn't know why anyone would kill his family.

But, there was no solid proof to tie Jeff to the crime. He was free to go. Nobody else was arrested since the clues ended there. The case remained cold for years.

Jeff relocated to Florida and got married. He was working as a teacher, and life was good for the now-30-year-old.

Then, in 2002, despite it being 13 years since the massacre, the cold case was brought up by St. Joseph County District Attorney Christopher Toth. Christopher was looking for re-election, but one of the biggest roadblocks he faced was his constituents' frustration that he'd refused to charge Jeff Pelley with murdering his family.

To retain his position as DA, he promised an indictment from the grand jury against Jeff. By August 2002, the suspect was once again arrested, but this time, he was actually charged with killing Bob, Dawn, Janel, and Jolene.

The evidence used to successfully charge - and eventually convict - Jeff was the same evidence the police had against him 13 years prior. No new evidence had come to light, just a rekindled desire to have the culprit jailed. In 2006, Jeff was handed 160 years in jail, 40 years for each killing.

However, Jeff still maintained his innocence. The evidence against him had only ever been circumstantial, however incriminating it may be. This has led to many people believing an innocent man was sent to prison.

In the spring of 2008, Jeff appealed his sentence and claimed that his defense attorneys had not adequately represented him in court. This was unsuccessful. Jeff would again appeal in 2023, telling the court that his previous attorneys didn't investigate any other potential suspects or theories about the murders. One theory was that Bob had been involved with some unsavory people.

Toni Beehler, a friend of Bob's who sold portraits of parishioners, told the police that the pastor had some ties with the "mob" in Florida. When he tried to distance himself from the organized crime he'd gotten himself entangled with, Toni said Bob became fearful of the criminals he once worked for. In her police interview, Toni suggested that the Pelley murders were acts of revenge by "the mob," who were angry when the pastor refused to continue moving their money.

Bob had previously worked in a bank, which was where he allegedly moved the money for the criminals. To distance himself from the dangerous men, he moved on, eventually becoming a well-respected pastor.

Toni recalled him telling her, "They are going to kill each member of my family," adding that he would be made to watch before they slaughtered him, too. Days after this conversion, the Pelleys were dead.

Still, none of this information had any effect on Jeff's position behind bars. He remains in Indiana State Prison and will be eligible for parole in January 2082. It's unlikely Jeff will live to see his eligibility date.

There are forums and websites dedicated to proving Jeff's innocence, with many people believing that Bob's past had caught up with him. It's an interesting but frustrating case since there is little concrete evidence against Jeff. At the same time, there is no solid evidence to guide law enforcement to another suspect, either.

To think a 17-year-old boy could slaughter his family and then go on a trip to a theme park is a frightening one. As is the idea that an innocent man went to jail for a quadruple murder he didn't commit. Either the former or the latter is true; which one do you believe?

The Unrepentant Ex

The details of this case are light, but the content of the case itself is incredibly heavy. It's the violent story of a jealous lover who took his possessive nature to extreme levels, carrying out a horrifying attack on his ex-girlfriend.

The culprit in this case is Zachary Gross. We can often tell a lot about someone from their surname: their cultural background, or where they're from. In this instance, Zachary's surname appears to be an apt descriptor not of his roots but of him. He was a domestic abuser, a controlling man who couldn't handle his ex-girlfriend deciding she no longer wanted him in her life.

Marilyn Stanley, from Kentucky, was 25 when she began dating Zachary. As with all abusive partnerships, it didn't begin that way. Marilyn was charmed and flattered by the 31-year-old and soon found herself falling for him. Like clockwork, that's when the abuse began. However, Marilyn wouldn't put up with her partner raising his hands to her. On average, it takes a woman seven attempts to leave an abusive partner before they succeed. Marilyn only had the opportunity to flee once before Zachary mutilated her irreversibly.

After ending the relationship, Zachary hadn't stopped contacting his ex. According to Marilyn, he became "obsessed." So much so that he even took it upon himself to get a job at the same warehouse where she worked. From the outside looking in, we can see where this ominous tale is heading. But Marilyn didn't ever imagine her ex had it in him to attack her the way he would.

After months of pestering and pleading with her to give him one more chance, Zachary finally convinced Marilyn to meet up with him in September 2015. Their prearranged meeting was to talk things over, or so Marilyn thought. In reality, the vengeful ex had seen a social media post that upset him greatly: another man had posted a picture of Marilyn to his social media feed.

If Marilyn and this man were dating, she had done no wrong: she was no longer in a relationship with Zachary. In fact, she'd been doing her best to detangle herself from his life. This fact appeared to be lost on Zachary.

When the exes met up at his home, he beat her mercilessly. It wasn't a quick attack by any means; it went on for over two hours. He beat, berated, and battered his ex while she tried to protect herself as best she could. Her attempts at shielding herself were in vain; Zachary wasn't relenting.

When he got tired of attacking the woman, he set his pit bull on her. The vile man commanded his heavyset dog to maul his ex, which saw Marilyn lose part of her ear.

This didn't sate the attacker. He discovered a folding knife Marilyn had brought with her for her own safety. Part of her knew her ex was going to lash out at her, so she attempted to arm herself with the knife just in case. She never got the chance to retrieve it; Zachary got to it first.

As Marilyn, beaten and defenseless, lay on the floor, her ex brutally took the blade to her scalp. He sliced her skin right down to the bone and removed her scalp from her head. Unbelievably, he then flung the bloody flesh into a plastic bag. Then, he demanded his victim lay on her side. He stomped down on her ribs until he was satisfied with audible cracks.

Zachary then bundled Marilyn into his car. He drove her to her mother's house and flung her out, not before handing her the plastic bag that contained her scalp. He also demanded a kiss from her before casting her from the vehicle.

Some of Zachary's last words to his victim were warning her that nobody else would ever want her now that she was bald.

Marilyn made her way into her mother's home, who was horrified at the sight of her severely beaten and bloodied daughter. "Here's a bag of my hair," she said to her mother, not realizing the content of the bag was, in fact, her scalp. An ambulance was called, and Marilyn was raced to hospital, still not fully grasping just how serious the attack on her had been. She'd blacked out during parts of it, which some may see as a small mercy.

The 25-year-old underwent emergency surgery, where it was found the woman had endured a severed artery in the attack. It was causing her to lose blood rapidly. Her face had multiple fractures. Her ribs also had a number of breaks.

When Marilyn came round from her surgery, the doctor came and told her the extent of her injuries. "Your hair isn't going to grow back," he told her bluntly. This shocked her; she'd been left with just the back and sides. Her once-thick hair had been reduced to covering just half of her head. While thankful she'd escaped with her life, Marilyn was a young woman who took pride in her appearance. She was bereft that her hair was never, ever going to grow back. She likened herself to being in a horror movie when she looked at herself for the first time.

Meanwhile, the police had caught up with Zachary Gross. He was charged with assault and kidnapping, charges he pleaded not guilty to. He asserted that he didn't attack Marilyn; his pit bull did. He said all of Marilyn's injuries, including the precise scalping, had been from his dog attacking her. When asked why he gave his brutalized ex a bag containing her scalp, Zachary claimed he was helping her.

He reiterated this story at his trial, too. Zachary said that he felt "horrible" for the injuries Marilyn sustained but claimed he wasn't responsible. "I maintain my innocence. It is what it is. I'm not asking for your mercy," he nonchalantly told the judge. "Just give me the 20. I don't need a lecture," he said brazenly.

The judge did, in fact, "give him the 20," plus some extra time for obscene gestures he gave to the news cameras during the trial. Zachary smirked his way through the whole thing, never showing one ounce of remorse or repentance.

The pit bull was put to sleep, and Zachary's four-year-old son was removed from his custody after the sentencing. The man's vile actions didn't just gravely affect a young woman's life, but they also infected the lives of those who were close to him.

Marilyn had to have subsequent surgeries due to nerve damage, her severed ear, and to reconstruct her face. She now has to wear wigs or a wool hat over her head. The survivor still suffers flashbacks and sometimes has nightmares about her ordeal, but she refuses to let it get the better of her.

Despite Zachary's warning that nobody would want her after he'd removed her scalp, Marilyn proved him wrong. She did indeed meet someone else. She already had a little boy called Carter from a previous relationship but also welcomed a girl called Evelyn and a boy called Storm with a new man who saw past Marilyn's injuries.

This case highlights some truly disturbing statistics when it comes to intimate partners and abuse. I recently wrote an article about battered woman syndrome, and the piece included some really sobering stats. Here are two of them:

One in four women has been severely assaulted by an intimate partner. The word severely refers to extreme assaults like punching, kicking, burning, strangulation, inflicting pain in sadistic ways, etc. This statistic is devastating enough, but it's made all the more dispiriting when you consider the next one:

Up to 75% of domestic homicides happen when the victim tries to leave their abuser. As terrifying as Zachary's attack was on Marilyn, the outcome could have been that she was part of the above percentage. Miraculously, she survived, but so many other women don't.

Baby-faced Killers

To comprehend the idea that, somewhere in the world, at some point in time, a teenage boy uttered the sinister phrase, "Why don't we get a girl and rape her?" is unfathomable. But they did. That sick phrase resulted in the death of an innocent woman in a horrifyingly brutal way.

If you've read *Unbelievable Crimes Volume Three*, you'll recall I covered the case of Anita Cobby, an Australian woman who was kidnapped, robbed, raped, and tortured before having her throat cut so badly she was almost decapitated. The case I'm about to cover - the murder of Janine Balding - has some cruel parallels to the shocking case of Anita Cobby.

Janine Balding was born on October 7, 1967, in a place called Wagga Wagga in New South Wales, Australia. When she was in her late teens, Janine moved to Sydney and took a job as a bank teller. The young woman's life was steadily becoming the life she'd dreamed of as a little girl; she had a job she enjoyed, she was engaged to be married, and she had just bought a home with her partner.

However, Janine and her fiancé, Steven, soon came to realize that weddings don't come cheap, especially if you want to have a lavish, family-filled ceremony. So, in order to save up the money to have the wedding they wanted, they rented their home out. It was a small, temporary price to pay for the pair to be able to exchange vows.

On September 8, 1988, Janine headed to work as usual. She would drive to Sydney's Sutherland train station and park her car there before departing to the city center for work. On her way home, at around 6 pm, she returned to her car only to be intercepted by five teenagers.

Teenagers on their own aren't much to be feared; you rarely get a lone teenager yelling obscenities at you or threatening you as you walk past them. However, their attitude can often change when they find themselves in a group. As does their threat level to innocent passersby.

Janine knew being approached by a gang of unkempt teenagers wouldn't bring anything good. All she wanted to do was get in the car, lock the doors, and drive home to safety.

That's exactly what Christine Moberley had done just moments earlier.

The homeless gang consisted of ringleader Bronson Blessington, who was just 14, Matthew Elliott, aged 16, Stephen "Shorty" Jamieson, who was 22 but hanging around with children; and 15-year-olds Wayne Wilmot and Carol Ann Arrow.

The gang had spent their day riding the trains, downing a bottle of rum Bronson had stolen earlier in the day, and crudely flashing a copy of an adult magazine at passersby. Bronson and Matthew had also allegedly taken amphetamines.

The group approached Christine as she entered her car, having already agreed among themselves to procure and rape a random victim.

Thankfully, Christine managed to lock herself in her car and evade capture from the feral teens. Before she drove out of the parking lot, she noticed the youths had moved on to another woman. The group was talking to this young woman beside a car, and it was clear she didn't know them. This made Christine feel uneasy.

Unbeknownst to her, the woman was Janine Balding. Feeling unsettled by the encounter, Christine called the police about the set of unruly teens bothering people at Sutherland train station. The police attended the area, only to head to the main car park of the train station. The youths had actually been targeting people at the overflow car park across the road, meaning officers narrowly missed the chance to stop the teens before they did something irreversible.

The gang initially got Janine's attention by stopping her to ask for the time. Then they asked for a spare cigarette, which escalated to them pressuring the young woman for money. In the end, one of the gang pulled out a knife and threatened to slash her face if she didn't comply with their demands. One of the teens then snatched her car keys, and the group bundled the terrified woman into the back of her own car.

The despicable teens drove the woman almost an hour to Minchinbury, a small suburb in western Sydney. For the entire duration of the ride, Janine suffered unimaginable cruelty at the hands of her captors. She was forced to strip and was beaten and repeatedly raped by Bronson, Matthew, and Stephen. All the while, the large knife the group had was held to the woman's face.

To imagine the fear and horrors Janine endured is sickening enough, but to know that the group warned her she wasn't getting out of it alive is a truly heartbreaking aspect of the case. Despite the horrific things she'd endured, at one point, Janine had hoped she would get out of her ordeal alive. That little glimmer of hope was snatched from her when the group audibly discussed how it was "a nice night for murder."

The group drove down the M4 motorway and looked for a suitable area to pull up. Eventually, they found a lane that was adjacent to some barren land. The teens pulled a beaten and terrified Janine from her car and violently shoved a scarf in her mouth to gag her. She was then tied up, and the three rapists sexually assaulted her again.

After they ceased attacking the woman, Bronson, Matthew, and Stephen dragged her to a dam nearby, breaking her wrist in the process. Once they made it to the water, they held her face down. The three brutes drowned her after subjecting her to multiple vile assaults.

The gang was not done yet. To add more insult to injury, they looted her lifeless body. They stole Janine's jewelry and her bank cards. Her PIN was folded up on a piece of paper inside her purse. They then got back in her car, which quickly broke down. The quintet walked back to the suburb of Mount Druitt, where they split up. Before they did, the corrupt youths went to town with Janine's money, withdrawing from several ATMs and selling her jewelry.

Bronson and Matthew told another homeless teen about the vile acts they'd just carried out before the pair retired for the night in a park. The following day, the duo stole a car and drove it to a youth center where Bronson would meet with his youth worker. For reasons unknown, he confessed to her that he'd brutally beaten another teen. The story was true - he and Matthew Elliot had attacked another boy days earlier and beat him mercilessly with a sledgehammer.

Surprisingly, the boy survived, but no culprits had been found - until now. The youth worker called the police, who spoke to the boys. It was at this point the two, entirely unprovoked, admitted that they knew Janine Balding had been raped and killed. At this point in time, the woman was only reported missing - her body hadn't been found. The strange confession caused the police to ask more questions. The woman had been abused, the teens said, but both boys insisted they didn't participate in it.

Their story was, at best, a cruel, sick joke they were playing. At worst, it was true, and these youngsters were the culprits. The more the boys talked, the more the latter was seemingly the case.

The police asked the pair to take them to Janine's body, which they did. She was partly submerged in the water they'd held her under. Bronson stared at the body, unfazed by the fact that he'd been party to the killing. He was fascinated that he was standing before a dead body, a surreal experience that didn't provoke any guilt or sorrow, just morbid fascination.

Janine's parents, Beverley and Kerry, and her fiancé, Mark, were informed of the finding. Their worst fears - and more - had been realized.

By now, the boys had divulged too much to the police to keep maintaining their innocence. They confessed all and gave the names of the other youths involved. All five were arrested and charged with the murder of Janine Balding.

Matthew Elliott, Bronson Blessington, and Stephen "Shorty" Jamieson were all found guilty and given life behind bars plus an additional 25 years. Bronson was the youngest of the convicted, being just 14 at the time. Still, that didn't stop the judge from remarking that none of the killers should ever be released. Youngsters or not, the crime they had carried out was so sick and severe that the judge felt unable to recommend they ever step foot on the streets again.

Wayne Wilmot and Carol Ann Arrow weren't sentenced as harshly. They aided in the kidnapping of Janine but didn't participate in the sexual assaults or the killing. Wayne spent almost eight years in jail before being released. Carol did just less than two years behind bars before being released. Nobody knows where she is, but she hasn't reoffended.

The same can't be said for Wayne Wilmot. In 1998, he was sent back to prison for a further seven years after the attempted abduction and rape of a young girl in Sydney. He had been free for only two years when he attacked the girl. He was also linked via DNA to the sexual assault of another teenager. He's been dubbed a "serial sex offender" and subsequently remains at Junee Correctional Centre.

He was initially due to be released in 2019, but his behavior inside prison and his lack of remorse and understanding of his crimes saw his release blocked. He's been deemed too much of a danger to women to release. A proposed release in 2023 was also rejected for this reason.

The three killers remain in maximum security jails.

As of 2024, Janine would have been 56 years old. Her parents and her younger brother were changed forever by her barbaric end, although the family tried their best to remember Janine as they knew her and to keep her memory alive.

Sadly, after over 25 years of heartache, Beverly died in October 2013. Her husband, Kerry, would pass away in 2022. They lay next to their Janine in Wagga Wagga Lawn Cemetery.

When asked about how he feels about his actions, Bronson Blessington says, "I'm really ashamed about what I did." He has allegedly found religion behind bars, and if he's ever released, he would like to set up a ministry to help young people.

If you've not read Volume Three of this series and you don't know of the Anita Cobby murder, I'd suggest looking it up online. You'll see it's eerily similar to this case, with a similar set of delinquents carrying out the killing. Though it's a disturbing case and a tough read, I will forewarn you.

Mind Control Killer

This case of a Japanese serial killer sounds entirely made up; it's so over-the-top and unbelievable you might think it's untrue. Sadly, it's a very real and very overlooked case that took place in the 1980s. It was so sick and twisted that the Japanese media refused to report it when Futoshi Matsunaga's spate of crimes was uncovered. As such, the facts and details surrounding this case are somewhat thin, but there's enough information out there to be able to piece together the morbid tale.

Futoshi Matsunaga was born on April 28, 1961, to a family that doted on him. Futoshi was encouraged academically and would become a top student in his classes. He was also popular among his peers, earning the class president title.

At home, he was seen as a golden child, but young Futoshi's veil of perfection soon slipped at school when his teachers caught him in a relationship with another pupil. On top of this, Futoshi would sometimes get angry or verbally abusive if his teachers tried to discipline him, and he was quickly transferred to another school.

Still, he graduated high school, and it looked like the young man had a bright future ahead of him. Futoshi got married at 19, and the young couple had a son together. However, Futoshi wasn't the settling-down type; he was known to flit from woman to woman and reportedly even managed to juggle ten mistresses at one point. From a young age, Futoshi had been able to charm women.

As a young boy, older women would be delighted by his polite nature and ability to partake in adult conversation. As a teen, his female peers would be captivated by his disregard for authority and were drawn in by his brash attitude, something that was uncommon in Japan. As an adult, he'd managed to perfect his smooth-talking with the opposite sex and was rarely rejected by the women he pursued.

The more you learn about Futoshi, the more you'll realize that he wouldn't handle rejection well at all.

There was no denying that Futoshi was incredibly clever and would likely have been successful at whatever career he chose. His father left him the family antique business, which Futoshi pivoted to selling only futons. And as you can imagine, he turned it into a lucrative venture. Futoshi bought a warehouse to hold all the stock and employed a number of workers to run the business.

However, his treatment of his employees was grotesque. The men would be busy at work, and Futoshi would run up behind them and administer electric shocks. He would taunt his victims, telling them there was a spirit behind them, sucking away at their fortune. In reality, it was Futoshi with his electric shock device.

While running the futon company, Futoshi still somehow managed to juggle all of his many mistresses. One of them was Junko Ogata, a woman with whom he'd gone to high school. She would outlast all of Futoshi's other women, something she'd pay a hefty price for.

Junko was born in February 1962, and after graduating, she decided she wanted to work with preschoolers. Her caring and tender nature saw her excel at her teaching job, and for a few years, Junko lived a normal, quiet life with her mother and father. That would soon change when she reconnected with Futoshi in 1982.

The 20-year-old would become enamored with Futoshi, something he used to his advantage. Her kind and placid nature meant she was easy to coerce and bully, and despite Futoshi's mistreatment of his girlfriend, she believed they would one day get married. She had no idea he was already wed, but even if she discovered this betrayal, it's likely Futoshi's silver tongue would see him talk his way out of it.

Junko's mother knew her daughter was being abused. The young woman still lived with her parents, and they saw a drastic change in their once-happy child. Shizumi Ogata begged her daughter to end the relationship, but Junko insisted she cared for her boyfriend, and he cared for her; they were going to get married, Junko asserted.

There was no way Shizumi was going to give the couple her blessing, and she told her daughter as much. This angered Futoshi, who took it upon himself to visit the Ogata household and punish the woman for her objection. He burst into the home and raped Junko's mother for daring to defy his wishes.

You would think this act severed Futoshi's relationship with Junko altogether. In fact, he used it as a tool to unify them. After the vile attack, he returned to Junko and persuaded her that her family hated her. He brought up a previous suicide attempt of Junko's and convinced her that her mother and father wanted her out of their lives because of this event. None of this was true, of course, but Junko was malleable when it came to Futoshi.

The only option was for Junko to run away with Futoshi. That's just what she did.

The physical and emotional abuse would only escalate from there. Where Junko had previously had her parent's home as a place of respite, she was now alone in the clutches of her abuser. The pair would have two sons together, but even the birth of his children wouldn't stop Futoshi's violent outbursts toward Junko.

His futon business was bringing in more and more money, and by his early 20s, Futoshi was a wealthy young man. However, the business was a front for his dealings with criminals and the yakuza. He'd managed to blackmail and con his business partners and customers out of 180 million yen, which, in the 80s, was a hefty sum of money. However, as clever as Futoshi was, the law would eventually catch up with him, and he was put on Japan's *Most Wanted* list, along with his "accomplice," Junko.

The pair went on the run, but this didn't quell Futoshi's desire to have many mistresses. One of his plethora of conquests was a woman whose identity remains unknown. The Japanese word for woman translates as "Onna," so that's what I'll call her from now on. Futoshi somehow managed to convince Onna that

Junko wasn't his lover but was his sister. On these pretenses, Onna agreed to run away with her lover in the spring of 1993, bringing her three children along. This made up a total of three adults and five children who were now on the run together.

Futoshi was violent and sadistic to his women, so you can surmise that he treated the children the same way. In September 1993, one of Onna's children suddenly died, the circumstances of which are unknown. However, her remaining two children were quickly sent to live with their father after this tragedy. Onna came to the realization that Futoshi's promises had been empty, and he didn't love her at all. He'd managed to swindle almost 12 million yen from her, which left her destitute.

It seems that Futoshi no longer saw any value in Onna, and her remains were found in the spring of 1994, one year after she'd left her husband to run away with the con man. Just like the death of her child, there was no evidence to connect Futoshi to the murder, and he wasn't pursued by the police for the killing. We still don't know exactly how or why Onna died, but it seems it triggered what would be the start of Futoshi's foray into murder.

While on the run, Futoshi still needed a way to generate an income. Getting a job simply wasn't an option for him, so he relied on his ability to defraud people of their hard-earned cash. He met Kumio Toraya while out drinking one night and managed to get the man to open up and confess about the illegal activities he'd participated in in the past. Kumio confessed to his new companion that he owed a lot of money to some unsavory people who were still on the hunt for him.

While Kumio perhaps felt he was letting off steam to a stranger, he was actually divulging information that could be used against him. Futoshi was all ears, listening to Kumio as he spoke of his deepest, darkest secrets. While Futoshi initially appeared sympathetic toward the man, he soon changed his tune. He threatened to use this information against Kumio if he didn't give in to his demand: he wanted to move into Kumio's apartment.

A strange demand, you may think, but Kumio felt he had no choice but to relent. His life depended on it. However, allowing Futoshi, his girlfriend, and his children to move in with him, signaled the beginning of the end for Kumio.

Kumio lived with his young daughter, whose name has never been revealed. I'll call her "Musume," which is Japanese for daughter. Pretty soon, Kumio's apartment became his very own torture den, where neither he nor his daughter would be allowed to set food outside. Futoshi forced Musume to abuse her own father, beating him and biting him at Futoshi's command. He even made the terrified girl feed her father his own waste - a truly sickening act that served to make Futoshi laugh.

Musume was also tortured by her captor, enduring horrific electrocutions and assaults at Futoshi's hands. When winter time came, which can often be freezing in Japan, the father and daughter were forced inside the apartment's bathroom and sprayed down with cold water. They were locked inside and left to endure the bitter temperatures together.

This went on for two whole years. Eventually, in 1996, aged just 34, Kumio succumbed to his injuries and died. Naturally, Futoshi blamed Musume for murdering her father. The child believed what her captor told her; after all, she was the one who'd electrocuted and beat her dad. Futoshi rarely needed to lift a finger during the torture sessions when he was able to coerce his victims to assault one another.

After convincing the child she'd killed her father, he told Musume that she needed to help dispose of the body. Together, they cut Kumio's body into pieces before boiling it in several pans. Disgustingly, Futoshi ordered Musume to drink some of the boiling water her father's body parts were cooking in.

Junko and Musume were ordered to clean up the bloody crime scene and dispose of the remains, which were bagged up and thrown into the sea.

Futoshi was still in need of money. He allowed Junko to get a job, which meant she was able to come and go from the apartment. Musume wasn't allowed to leave unless Futoshi accompanied her.

Remarkably, Junko would go to work and come straight home, never seeking help or alerting anyone to what her partner had been doing for years behind closed doors. Perhaps it was Stockholm syndrome, or perhaps Junko had become so desensitized she believed this was her new normal. Either way, her inability to seek help enabled Futoshi to continue his reign of terror.

It didn't take long for the wicked man to find new prey. Again, it was a woman with a child, and again, he managed to convince her that he loved her and that he'd marry her. He again introduced Junko as a relative and claimed that Musume was his niece. Once he got his claws into the woman and got 5.6 million yen out of her, she found herself trapped inside the apartment Futoshi was passing off as his own. The woman was subject to beatings and electrocutions until, in March 1997, she jumped out of the two-story window to escape. After being taken to hospital, she told the police everything.

However, by the time law enforcement got to the apartment, Futoshi, Junko, and Musume were long gone.

Futoshi's sadism hadn't even scratched the surface yet.

That same year, after 15 years under Futoshi's dark spell, Junko began to feel disenchanted with her partner. Where she would once have done anything he told her to, she was getting tired of all the death and chaos that surrounded her life. So, one morning, on her way to work, she decided to flee the relationship. When Junko didn't return home that night, Futoshi set about looking for her. The first place he went was Junko's parents' home, and her mother answered the door. This was the same woman he'd raped almost 15 years prior. The word brazen doesn't quite cut it.

As you can imagine, when he turned up at Junko's parents, her mother refused to tell Futoshi where her daughter was. The mother stood her ground and refused to disclose Junko's location, no matter how much pressure the abusive man put on her. Futoshi even told Shizumi that Junko was a murderer, and if she didn't tell him where she was hiding, he'd bring the police to the apartment and have them all arrested. The protective parent would not relent, meaning Futoshi had no choice but to leave.

However, Futoshi wasn't the type to just let Junko go. She was his property, and he would go to extreme lengths to make sure he lured her out of hiding. So, he faked his own death.

The trap was set when Futoshi leaked information that he'd killed himself, even arranging a fake funeral for himself. This elaborate scheme was supposed to allow Junko to feel safe enough to return home. After Futoshi's "funeral," Junko did, in fact, come out of hiding and went back to her parent's home as predicted.

Futoshi stalked Junko the whole time, and when the time was right, he went to her parent's property and surprised them by proclaiming he was "back from the dead." He brought young Musume along with him, too, another victim of his he was unwilling to set free. Devastated to discover their daughter's abuser was back on the scene, Junko's parents offered Futoshi over 60 million yen to leave them alone. The criminal agreed to the deal but, as you can probably guess, didn't keep his end of the bargain.

Instead, he held them hostage in their own apartment, just like he had with Kumio and Musume. This time, though, he had more captives: inside the apartment were Junko's mother and father, her sister Rieko, Reiko's husband, their two children - and, of course, Junko and Musume. That's eight captives to contend with.

Initially, you may think that eight individuals could, perhaps quite easily, have overpowered Futoshi and subdued him until law enforcement arrived. This was my initial thought, too; why didn't they band together to fight off their attacker? The captives' wrists were bound, but surely there was strength in numbers.

But, this underestimates Futoshi's ability to divide and conquer. His dark ability to coerce and persuade was so immense that he controlled every household member like a puppet. Eventually, his captives began to see Futoshi as their leader, and he inadvertently created a small cult for himself.

Junko's sister found herself under Futoshi's spell and soon began an intimate relationship with him. Again, you can perhaps chalk this behavior down to Stockholm syndrome; Rieko was doing what she thought she had to do to survive.

In December 1997, as he had done multiple times before, Futoshi ordered Junko to administer electric shocks to her father. The 61-year-old wouldn't be able to tolerate the persistent torture, and he died an agonizing death at the hands of his daughter. After this, Shizumi's mental health saw a rapid decline. The brutal death of her husband, coupled with the unbearable torture she was also subjected to, rendered her incapable of conversing. Instead, she would mumble in a strange voice, something that began to annoy Futoshi.

So, he ordered Rieko and her husband, Kazuya, to hold the woman down and strangle her to death. By now, Futoshi had emptied all of his captives' bank accounts. He didn't truly want the cult he'd created; he wanted to move on to the next batch of prey. So, he decided the captives had to die.

He ordered Rieko's daughter to pin her mother's arms down while Kazuya strangled her to death. Afterward, Kazuya was locked in the cold, damp bathroom with no food, water, or light. He would never be let out, despite his pleas. For two months, he sustained himself by drinking water out of the toilet bowl. Eventually, he succumbed to starvation.

The remaining victims were Junko, Musume, and Rieko's little boy and girl. Still, that was too many for Futoshi. He ordered Junko and Musume to kill them, which they did via electrocution and strangulation. By now, it was summer 1998, and the trio set about dismembering and getting rid of the bodies that had piled up in the apartment.

Musume was desperate to escape her abuser. She'd seen and done too much, and if she had the chance to escape, she was going to take it. She knew Futoshi would try to track her down, but unlike Junko, she planned to go to the police and tell them everything. In 2002 - five years after the Ogata family massacre

- she managed to run away. She didn't succeed in getting to the police station; Futoshi found her and dragged her back to the apartment, torturing her for daring to leave.

Junko was ordered to inflict some of the more sickening abuse carried out on the youngster, including ripping her toenails off. Despite being beaten and battered, this only served to make Musume even more determined she was going to make it out alive. She made a break for it yet again shortly after, and this time, she was successful. Musume made it to the police station and told them everything. The police caught up with Futoshi and Junko the following day, and the pair were arrested.

Junko corroborated what Musume had told the police. She admitted her part in the murders and cooperated with the investigation. Futoshi denied all of the allegations against him. Again, it seems he felt his silver tongue would help him get out of this predicament. For the first time, possibly in his life, Futoshi had to face up to the idea that there was no way of talking himself out of this one.

The pair were charged with the murder of Reiko's children, the murder of Junko's mother and father, as well as her sister and brother-in-law.

Junko pleaded guilty, while Futoshi insisted it was Musume and Junko who carried out the killings and were conspiring against him. In the end, the courts saw through Futoshi's lies and sentenced him and Junko to death.

On appeal, Junko had her sentence reduced to life behind bars.

Due to her young age at the time she was kidnapped and because she was coerced to partake in the torture, Musume faced no charges for her involvement.

Futoshi remains in jail to this day, awaiting his fate. We can only shudder to think how many victims he would have racked up if his young victim hadn't managed to escape. An even more sinister thought is the idea that there are victims out there who were never identified. After all, Futoshi flitted about from city to city while on the run, and his choice of victim always allowed him to remain off the police's radar.

The Opportunist

Jessica Keen was a fun-loving teen from Columbus, Ohio. The 15-year-old honor student had her whole life ahead of her. She was a prominent cheer squad member who rarely got poor grades and got along well with her classmates.

However, as with most teens, Jessica would go through a rebellious phase. The once cheerful girl became withdrawn and sullen, and the animal-loving teens' dreams of becoming a zoologist were diminishing with her grades.

Her sudden change in demeanor coincided with her relationship with 18-year-old Shawn Tompson. The older boy had gone to the same school as Jessica, but the age gap was troubling for the girl's parents. Three years when you're an adult is nothing, but it can make all the difference when you're still developing. Her parents were desperate for her to break it off with the young man, not just because of the age gap but because it seemed to trigger her lack of interest in school.

In the spring of 1991, Jessica and her mother Rebecca were, once again, butting heads over the teenager's boyfriend. The protective parent had forbidden her daughter from meeting up with Shawn. In order to reason with Jessica, the mother promised she would lift the ban on the relationship if the girl could get her grades to an acceptable level again. After all, if she wanted to work with animals, she was going to need that scholarship.

It had come to Rebecca's attention that her daughter had been skipping classes to meet her boyfriend. Jessica had even quit the cheerleading team to spend her free time with Shawn. She was becoming less and less interested in anything but her relationship. Rebecca knew she had to do something drastic to get her child back on the right track.

Desperate, the Keen parents looked for help. They came across a counseling center for teenagers, which led to the decision to place Jessica in a two-week program at a place called Huckleberry House. The program would see the teenager participate in daily therapy sessions, and theoretically, by the fortnight's end, she would have her priorities straight again.

Jessica's bags were packed at the beginning of March, and she was dropped off at Huckleberry House for her live-in therapy. It also served to give the mother and child some breathing space from one another. They'd had an intense few months of arguments, and a break was just what they needed.

Jessica dove into the program, and it appeared she was open to the counselor's advice. The two weeks flew by quickly, and on March 15, Rebecca was looking forward to welcoming her daughter back. It was the day before she was due to arrive home, and Jessica made one last phone call to Shawn before she left Huckleberry House. Nobody knows what was said during the call - perhaps Jessica had decided to cool things or told him she needed space - but it didn't go well.

When the phone call ended, Jessica was visibly upset and frustrated. She told witnesses they'd broken up before taking off from Huckleberry House. She told a friend she was going to the mall and headed out to the bus stop nearby. This was at around 6 pm, but Jessica wouldn't return to the house that night.

The following day, she was reported missing. The police embarked on a thorough search of the area, finding nothing. Her last known presence was at the bus stop. From what they could piece together, Jessica never made it to the mall. Had she run away, or could someone have picked her up at the bus stop?

Tragically, almost two days after she vanished, Jessica's body was discovered. She was found 20 miles away from Huckleberry House in a graveyard. She was naked, apart from a sock and her bra. Her hands were bound with tape, and her mouth still had the gray tape tightly stuck over her lips. She'd clearly been beaten, though it was apparent that the cause of death was likely a blow to the head. The gravestone that was used to smash over Jessica's skull lay nearby. The force of the blow caused the gravestone to break in two.

In a sickening discovery, Jessica had been raped. The police managed to piece the evidence together to create a timeline of her final moments.

She had been sexually assaulted between two to four hours prior to her death. She was still wearing all of her jewelry when her body was found, besides one necklace that had the word "taken" etched onto it. This felt like a telling clue for investigators.

The cemetery offered various pointers as to what happened to Jessica the night she was killed.

The police were certain she'd been abducted in a car and that this was where the sexual assaults took place. Then, when Jessica saw the opportunity, she fled, racing through the unlit country roads and ending up in a graveyard.

Following the muddied footprints, investigators could see the teenager had tried to evade her rapist by hiding behind large gravestones. She crouched down and left her knee prints behind the graves where she sought cover. As she was running through the mud, she lost a sock, which perhaps aided her attacker in finding her.

Jessica raced as fast as she could in the pitch black, eventually hurtling into a fence. The speed at which she was running caused the impact to render Jessica immobile. She fell to the ground, where her attacker found her. He lifted up a nearby gravestone and smashed it down onto the teenager's head.

The first suspect police pinpointed was Jessica's boyfriend, Shawn. Not only had they argued moments before she vanished, but her beloved "taken" necklace had also been snatched from her as a sick memento. Shawn insisted he didn't do it and seemed as devastated as you'd expect a love interest to be. He had an alibi: he'd been in Florida the night Jessica was killed. The police spoke to Shawn's group of friends, too. His alibi checked out, so they asked him to supply them with a sample of his DNA. He obliged, and the results proved he didn't rape Jessica. The one and only suspect the police had was now clear.

The case went cold. There was no more evidence to gather and no more suspects to look into. As with all cold cases, the crime was revisited over the years, with many investigators doing their best to snare the killer and finally close the case.

Meanwhile, Jessica's mother was beside herself. She blamed herself despite doing what she thought was best for her child. Rebecca prayed her daughter's killer would be caught; at least that way, the family - and Jessica - could get a small amount of closure.

In 2008, 17 years after Jessica's murder, there was a glimmer of hope. Sheriff Jim Sabin had been tasked with taking another look into the case. Over the years, many a Sheriff or detective had been given the same task, and each of them vowed to catch the killer. Sadly, none of them would be able to take the case any further. However, this time was different: it seems they found a match for the semen sample taken from Jessica's body.

The sample had been put through a program called CODIS, which stands for Combined DNA Index System. The software holds local, state, and national databases of DNA profiles from convicted offenders and unsolved crime scene evidence.

The hit led detectives to Marvin Lee Smith Jr. Marvin's brushes with the law had always been down to his abuse of women, so the police were beyond sure this was their guy. The evening Jessica was killed, Marvin was out on bail from another crime involving sexual abuse.

Naturally, a serial sex offender is unlikely to stop, especially if they've gotten away with it. After Jessica's murder, he resumed his depraved ways and found himself in jail yet again. Upon his 2000 release, he was ordered to give a DNA sample, which had become mandatory by that point. It took until 2008 for the semen from Jessica's body to be run through CODIS, thus finally bringing up a match.

With the weight of evidence against him, there was no way Marvin could deny he'd raped and killed Jessica. In his 2009 trial, he confessed to being the killer, which saw the death penalty option removed from his sentencing. He was handed 30 years to life and remains in Warren County, Ohio, where he's not eligible for parole until 2038.

Jessica's mother has struggled to forgive herself in the aftermath of her daughter's murder. She thinks about the teenager running for her life in the graveyard and says she can feel her racing heart as she tried in vain to flee her killer. Rebecca says she imagines Jessica praying behind the tombstones as her attacker was trawling the graveyard for her.

However, the only person in this case who ought to be asking for forgiveness isn't Rebecca; it's Marvin Lee Smith Jr.

Death on the Beach

This is the tragic tale of a couple who were murdered just before they were due to get married. Lindsay Cutshall, 22, and her fiancé Jason Allen, 26, were coldly slaughtered as they enjoyed time together on a romantic beach date. Would justice ever be served, or would this be a frustrating case that saw the killer evade the law?

Lindsay and Jason were two outdoor enthusiasts who bonded over their mutual love for nature and their equally strong faith in God. After five months of dating, Jason proposed, and it was a no-brainer for Lindsay; she didn't need to be asked twice. Their big day was scheduled for September 2004. Prior to their upcoming nuptials, they made plans to have their last summer as fiancés in El Dorado County, California, working as counselors at a Christian camp.

They wouldn't live to see their wedding day.

Lindsay had grown up in Fresno, Ohio. Her parents were devout Christians, and Lindsay was raised the same way. She was homeschooled and dreamed of becoming a missionary when she was older. After she graduated, she went to Appalachian Bible College to participate in spiritual outreach by taking part in outdoor activities. Lindsay was an avid lover of the outdoors, so partaking in whitewater rafting or abseiling appealed to her greatly.

Here, she'd meet Jason Allen.

Jason had grown up in Michigan in an equally religious family. He was a little older than Lindsay and had already attended Appalachian Bible College years prior. In 2002, he headed back there to work with the students and offer his guidance to them. When he was introduced to Lindsay Cutshall, it was as close to love at first sight as you can get for the pair.

They each told their respective families about the relationship, and eventually, the couple would meet one another's parents. Each side of the family was happy with their child's choice of partner. Jason got on extremely well with his girlfriend's parents. So much so, after five months of dating, he asked Lindsay's father, Chris Cutshall, for her hand in marriage. The traditional gesture was well received by the proud dad, and Lindsay said yes straight away.

The pair were inseparable and even got work at the same place, *Rock 'N' Water*, a Christian summer camp in California. While here, they made the most of the nature that surrounded them. They took the youth on outings in the woods, guided them on hikes, taught them how to whitewater raft, and tutored them in rock climbing. The days were as much fun for Lindsay and Jason as they were for the children they were leading.

Their evenings were spent with one another, having sunset walks and enjoying home-cooked meals. It was a perfect summer for the loved-up couple in the lead-up to their big day, which they were greatly looking forward to.

By the time August 2004 rolled by, the couple were just one month away from becoming man and wife, and their season at the Christian camp was coming to an end. For their last weekend in California, the pair decided to drive just over two hours to San Francisco, where they intended to be tourists for a couple of nights. They were due back at the camp by the late afternoon of August 15, 2004. They wouldn't show up.

Every Sunday, Lindsay had got into the habit of calling her mother and giving her a rundown of her week, letting her know the highs and lows of being a camp counselor. Kathy waited by the phone for her daughter's call, which would never arrive. This panicked the mother, who knew Lindsay wouldn't miss their weekly chats. She knew something was wrong.

When Monday came around, and there was still no call from Lindsay, it was all but confirmed something bad had happened. The Cutshalls booked a ticket and flew from Ohio to the camp in California, where they discovered Lindsay and Jason hadn't been seen for days. They didn't turn up for their shift on Monday, either. The police were called immediately.

Around the same time, a park ranger was doing his rounds in Fish Head Beach in Jenner, which is about an hour and a half north of San Francisco. He noticed a red car had been parked there all weekend. It was unusual, so he noted the license plate and alerted the authorities, just in case there'd been reports of someone going missing.

He also decided to make his way down the embankment near where the car was abandoned and head toward the beach. He wanted to make sure the driver hadn't had an accident in the water or on the sand and was unable to make it back to their vehicle. What he'd find would be much, much worse.

Initially, he saw what looked like two people taking a nap in a sleeping bag. The closer he got to them, the more ominous it felt that they weren't moving. Finally, he got close enough to ascertain that the people in the sleeping bag were dead. Their heads each had a single bullet hole.

The police were alerted, and a search of the crime scene took place. The backpacks beside the deceased man and woman provided officers with a positive ID of the couple. It was Lindsay Cutshall and Jason Allen.

At first glance, it looked like a murder-suicide. Perhaps they were star-crossed lovers, or one of the couple had slaughtered the other before shooting themselves. However, upon further inspection, there was no gun at the scene, nor were there any casings left behind. It was a cold-blooded murder. *But why*?

Neither individual had been sexually assaulted, nor did it appear their bodies had been tampered with after their murder. Their belongings hadn't been taken. It seems the killer had cruelly shot them once in the head and taken off. As hard as police looked, they simply couldn't find a motive. Lindsay and Jason didn't have any enemies. They were known as a free-spirited, laid-back couple who got on with everybody they met.

A nearby disposable camera offered investigators a glimpse into the couple's final hours alive. They'd enjoyed time walking along the coast, had spent time in the city center, and posed for the typical Golden Gate Bridge picture every tourist gets.

Receipts from the couple's bag show they bought some hot sauce and visited a surf shop. They had a conversation with the surf shop owner about places to rent a room, which led them to Fish Head Beach. It's been suggested that the couple ended up sleeping here after being unable to rent a motel room.

News of the crime was now circulating, leading a woman to contact the police with a potential tip. She was suspicious of her boyfriend, Shaun Gallon. As she put it, he had a history of "doing weird things." There's a big difference between "weird" and "murderer," but the police ran with the tip and visited his property.

He was already well-known to authorities, having been arrested multiple times for drug use. He was also a die-hard survivalist and prepper, and even the police described him as being "alternative." When they arrived at his home, they found frozen animals in his freezer from hunting and any number of guns and bulletproof vests. Despite Shaun being an odd character, the police had nothing to arrest him for.

A large cash reward was offered for any evidence that led to the prosecution of the killer, which meant people were forthcoming with tips. None of them, however, led to anything. Over a decade had passed, and the case was as cold as ever.

Then, in 2017, someone called in a shooting at a private property - it was Shaun Gallon's home. He'd fatally shot his brother. Shaun, full of rage for reasons still unknown, took his rifle and blasted shot after shot toward his brother, killing his 36-year-old sibling. He confessed to the killing straight away - there was really no way he could deny it - which led the police to once again question him about the murders of Lindsay Cutshall and Jason Allen.

Still, Shaun denied any involvement. To get the police off his back, he agreed to take a lie detector. When asked the questions regarding the Fish Head Beach killings, he failed spectacularly.

Still, this wasn't enough to charge Shaun with anything, but it did make the police take a closer look at him as the potential double killer. So, they obtained a search warrant for his home and computer. A deep dive into his computer history and social media pages showed that he was heavily into satanism and the occult. Then, there was an eyebrow-raising comment from the same girlfriend who'd called the police on him years prior. It read: "Maybe I should just go turn you in for that 50 grand reward?"

The evidence wasn't doing Shaun any favors. While the police were still investigating his involvement, and he was pending trial for the murder of his brother, Shaun admitted he was the one who'd slaughtered the sleeping couple. He told officers that he'd been hunting boar on Fish Head Beach when he saw the young couple sleeping on the beach. He shot Jason first, which caused Lindsay to wake up suddenly. He then murdered the startled woman.

His reason for the cold, callous slayings? He didn't like the fact that the couple were camping on the beach. It was a most unbelievable story. So much so that the police actually started to become dubious that the admittedly strange man was telling them the truth. But, the more they questioned him, the more information was divulged. Shaun admitted to picking up his spent shell casings before hiding them on his father's land.

Officers went to Shaun's dad's property and found the casings in a blackberry bush, just like Shaun said they would be. It took 13 years, but the police had finally snared the killer.

Shaun Gallon would end up pleading guilty to the double murder alongside the killing of his younger brother. He was given three life terms for the despicable crimes.

The Cutshalls and the Allens no doubt felt relief that the killer was no longer running free to hurt anybody else. It's just a shame that he was able to take another victim before the police eventually got him.

Final Thoughts

Thank you for reading the ninth installment of *Unbelievable Crimes*.

Researching some of these crimes has caused me to pause and close my laptop while I digested what I'd just learned. How people can be so brutal and cruel to another human is beyond me. How people can gain enjoyment from the suffering of others is just incomprehensible.

I had three more cases planned for this installment, each of them remaining partly written and unfinished. However, the details of these crimes were just terrible - as are the details of all crimes - but these cases were especially horrific to learn about.

At times, it felt like I was writing a gory extreme horror novel, not recounting the tragic final few moments of a murder victim. The intricate but important details in these cases, I felt, were just too gruesome to include. Despite having a trigger warning at the beginning of this book and in the description, I don't feel like there was any warning strong enough for these cases.

As such, I made the decision not to include them in this volume, although I may include them in future volumes. Anything that involves children can be particularly hard-hitting, and these crimes were prime examples of cases that make you simmer with anger. If I'd included the disturbing cases I didn't finish writing up, you'd be reading one gory, disturbing true story after another without a break. It would have been too much.

I always try to maintain a balance in the stories I cover. When a case sees the killer get away with it, I like to follow a story where the culprit faces justice. When I cover a cold case, I like to counter it with a case that was solved. I try to keep things balanced so you, the reader, don't get fatigued or frustrated by the book's content. Cold case after cold case can get frustrating after a while.

This brings me to my next point: what kind of cases do you like to read? If a case is particularly disturbing, would you still like it included in the anthology with a warning beforehand?

It reminds me of reading my mother's true crime books years ago. She had shelves full of them - books dedicated to Jack the Ripper and true-life tales of child abuse written by the survivor. Back then, nothing had trigger warnings. Now, we have it before a TV show that depicts a potentially triggering topic or scene.

Anyway, before I knew it, nine-year-old me had ingested hand-drawn images of the things Jack had done to his victims and gore-riddled descriptions of his crimes. A trigger warning perhaps would have been appreciated by younger me - though I'm unsure if my nine-year-old self would have actually heeded those warnings anyway. Morbid curiosity is something that humans develop from an early age, it seems.

Some readers appreciate my delving into the more gruesome, heinous cases. Others prefer certain details to be left out, but I personally feel it would do a disservice to the victim and their suffering if I did that. Again, let me know your thoughts on this.

As always, I'd like to thank you for your readership; it truly means a lot to me. I know so many of you jump from one volume to the next, and it warms me to know that. I enjoy researching and compiling these volumes, so thank you for enabling me to write them.

I hope I've covered some cases you'd not heard of and introduced you to stories you'd otherwise not have learned about. If you find the time to leave a review of this installment, that would be incredibly helpful to me, and I'd be extremely grateful. If you enjoyed this book, Volume Ten is in the works, and I'm also making plans to launch a new series, so stay tuned!

Once again, thank you for reading. Take care, and I'll leave you with a phrase that has become this series' mantra: *Always expect the unexpected.*

Daniela

You can sign up to my newsletter here:

<u>danielaairlie.carrd.co</u>[1]

Also by Daniela Airlie

Infamous Crimes

Infamous Cults: The Life and Crimes of Cult Leaders and Their Followers

Unbelievable Crimes

Unbelievable Crimes Volume One: Macabre Yet Unknown True Crime Stories

Unbelievable Crimes Volume Two: Macabre Yet Unknown True Crime Stories

Unbelievable Crimes Volume Three: Macabre Yet Unknown True Crime Stories

Unbelievable Crimes Volume Four: Macabre Yet Unknown True Crime Stories

Unbelievable Crimes Volume Five: Macabre Yet Unknown True Crime Stories

Unbelievable Crimes Volume Six: Macabre Yet Unknown True Crime Stories

Unbelievable Crimes Volume Seven

Unbelievable Crimes Volume Eight

Unbelievable Crimes Volume Nine
Unbelievable Crimes Volume Ten: Macabre Yet Unknown
True Crime Stories

Printed in Great Britain
by Amazon

42395529R00066